Erna's Medley

by

Ruby Paull

Brightest Pebble
Publishing Co. Inc.
1998

First Printing, April 1998 by:
Art Design Printing Inc., Edmonton, Alberta, Canada

Cover design by Art Design

First published in 1998 by:
Brightest Pebble Publishing Co. Inc.
P.O. Box 4218
Edmonton, Alberta, Canada
T6E 4T2
Phone (403) 435-5827 Fax (403) 435-5852

Canadian Cataloguing in Publication Data

Paull, Ruby, 1939-
Erna's medley

ISBN 0-9683627-0-2

1. Maron, Erna 2. Germans—Alberta—Veteran Region—Biography. I. Title.

FC3700.G3Z7 1998 971.23'3 C98-900445-7
F1080.G3P38 1998

Contents

ACKNOWLEDGMENTS

To Mother:

MRS. ERNA MARON.

Who, at age eighty-six, related her life story to us.

So that others might be informed of past truths.

So that others might learn from her experiences.

So that others might know that in the midst of turmoil and trials, God is there and life is good.

I am especially indebted to my sister Linda Maron for her valuable assistance in producing this book. Thanks also to James Musson for his help in editing the final manuscript.

Ruby Paull

Chapter 1

Born - A Village and a Baby.

In 1908, excitement filled the residents of a newly established German village in the Caucuses region of Russia. The village was named Morgintau — a German name.

Russia over the years had recruited many foreigners to immigrate to Russia to help build the country. German people made up a large part of the immigration, resulting in the establishing of many German sectors and villages.

German volunteers from nearby villages, called the Mother Colonies, built Morgintau.

It was required that at least sixty families consent and sign up to begin a new village. The papers for Morgintau had received permission from the governmental authority to go-ahead. After the new settlers obtained the necessary documentation, they began building their houses, sheds, and other buildings before making the final move.

The new residents were wealthy and their houses, built from the soil, were spacious and attractive.

Dirt, straw, chaff, and water were mixed together by horses trampling it until the proper consistency was reached. The mixture was then placed into wooden forms, which had been dipped in water. The forms were about one foot high, one foot wide, and two feet long. After the mud dried in the sun, it was removed from the form as a solid building adobe brick, similar to those made by the Israelites when they were slaves in Egypt, except for the fact that the Israelites did not have horses, or machinery to help them.

Roofing was made of a more substantial material—a form of brick made with stone. They were interlocked to fit and overlap. The finished house could stand up to the harshest elements.

The village completed, the people settled into their new homes with hearts full of joy and anticipation for the future. They were a hard working people who trusted in God to guide them in their lives.

Jochan Wiest, not only had a farm, but wealth too from raising and training oxen for sale. It takes a lot of knowledge and skill to properly train a team of oxen for field work. He had this knowledge and skill, along with a good head for business.

Jochan's wife Katherine was pregnant with Erna, the subject of this book and the author's mother. There were already eight children in the family — five boys and three girls. Families, at that time, were commonly large. Children were a welcomed asset, as many hands were needed to carry out family businesses. There would have been ten children in Jochan's family but two boys died, one at birth. There were no doctors near by, so midwives filled the vacancy and assisted mothers as best they could.

Villages were self-contained, having their own stores, shops, a school, a church, and other required establishments. These were run by the people in the village. The school was required to hire a Russian teacher to teach the children the Russian language. Apart from this, there were no restrictions on what was taught. The children became fluent in German and Russian. The church was Lutheran.

Jochan's brother, who also moved to this new village, had a vineyard. This was not unusual. Everyone in the area had a vineyard. What was unusual was that he invented a large oven to dry his grapes and thus produced the first raisins known to anyone there and he made a fortune on them. Erna, as a child, ate so many that to this day she can't stand the sight of them.

Their wine was called sweet wine and was not fermented. The juice was boiled and processed so as to keep for a long time. Everyone drank it, including the children.

The day of Erna's birth dawned bright and beautiful.

Elizabeth, the family's oldest girl, emerged from her mother's room shouting orders like a master sergeant,

"It's time, it's time!" Her shouts echoed throughout the household. "Someone get the midwife, quick! and, get dad! The bedding, the bedding, bring the bedding, the rags. Put the water on to boil, hurry!"

Frantic, children rushed to assist their mother. They knew what was about to happen and what their part would be in the long awaited drama. But when that final event was about to happen, excited minds became confused as to exactly what to do. Fortunately it was not long before the midwife arrived, followed by their dad. He came through the door with long rapid strides and a big smile that reassured the children that all would be well. The smile was for them only. Inside he was full of anxiety. The birth would not be easy. Katherine had already lost one child at birth, and she was now in her late forties—not a good time in life to be having a baby.

The midwife had expertly taken over, shooing the children out of the bedroom. Only Elizabeth was allowed to stay and assist. She was 16. As Jochan approached Katherine's bedside, she smiled at him through her pain, and reached for his hand. He took it and held it firmly, assuring her of his presence.

Preparation went quickly. The midwife was experienced and everything fell in place. Then came the waiting. This was the hardest part. Nothing more could be done to help, except encourage the one giving birth. A cold cloth on her forehead, her back rubbed, words of encouragement, all carried out by husband, midwife, and daughter.

The children on the other side of the door became anxious. An hour seemed like ten. They tried to peek in the door, only to have it slammed in their faces, as Elizabeth rushed through to get more water. Grunts and cries of pain could be heard as she then tripped over the sprawling bodies in front of her. All looked up to see the silhouette of their dad framed in the doorway.

"What's going on here?"

"These kids were trying to look in the door."

Jochan glared at them. "For shame!"

They hung their heads in embarrassment. "Well, we just wanted to see how things were going, if the baby is coming soon."

"That's impossible for anyone to see, but it will probably get here faster if you all get to work. Lots of things around here need doing."

Quickly the three of them got to their feet. Elizabeth continued on her way for the water, the others to find some tasks needing attention.

By putting their minds and bodies to work, time went faster. Then they heard a baby cry.

"It's here!"

"Wow--ee--ee!"

"Hooray!"

"Finally!"

They rushed to the door, listening quietly, to see if they could hear if everything was all right. Was it a girl or a boy? Knowing their concerns, their dad did not leave them waiting in suspense for long. The door opened and he announced the news.

"It's a girl!"

Erna was the first baby born in the new village.

One by one, two by two, little by little, the people of the village came to pay their respects to the first baby born in their village. They brought gifts, large and small, which were opened with reverence and appreciation.

The family was thrilled. It gave them a great distinction — a mark of honor, that would not be forgotten. The children were put to work baking, making lunch and treats for their visitors. No one left without first eating and enjoying a visit.

The baby, of course, was the center of attention. The rest of the children proudly, and with great enthusiasm, showed her off. But the new arrival had not yet been given a name. This became the concern of some very serious discussions. Everyone, including some of the visitors, came up with names .

Eventually the parents announced that the name would be Erna.

Erna is a Norwegian name, but it comes from the North Germanic language of Norway. Everyone was delighted..

The children argued incessantly as to who would take care of Erna.

"It's my turn."

"No, it's not, it's my turn."

"Lisa, it's my turn to care for the baby now!"

"Lisa, they're not being fair." Lisa was their name for Elizabeth.

"Would you guys be quiet. Your going to wake mom."

Her warning came too late, or perhaps the mom had not been asleep.

"If you kids are going to fight over the baby, you can just bring her back to me," insisted Katherine.

Dead silence. Then Elizabeth answered.

"It's okay mom. We'll sort it out. You just rest."

Katherine felt poorly. She seemed to be running a fever. The family was making out quite well, but she was irritable, easily annoyed and angered. Impatient and restless, she wanting to get up. But in those days, new mothers were not allowed to get out of bed right after a birth. Lack of knowledge and medical help made it dangerous. Should something go wrong, a doctor was a long ways away if there was one available at all. It was best not to take chances.

But Katherine had a large family. There was so much to be done, and she felt like she just couldn't stay in bed another minute. Besides, she was an old hand at having babies, wasn't she? So she got up and padded softly to the kitchen. Everyone turned to stare at her.

"Mom, you're not supposed to be up!" demanded Elizabeth. "Here, let me help you back to bed."

"Oh no your not. I'm tired of lying in that old bed. I don't think it helps at all; just makes you feel more sick and weak. I need to get moving. Get my strength back."

"But mom, the midwife said..."

"Never mind what she said. I know as much as she does."

They all knew there was no point in arguing. Besides, secretly they felt a bit relieved. Now things would get back to normal — at least as normal as possible with a new baby in the house.

Over the next couple of days Katherine set to work with a will, trying to forget that she didn't feel well. Why was she feeling so sick? She was so hot all the time. She tried drinking lots of tea, water, and juice but it didn't seem to help, and she just didn't feel like eating.

It was her lack of appetite that caught Jochan's attention. Try as she might, she just couldn't eat. Every bite made her feel like throwing up. Jochan squinted as he sat examining her pale, drawn face.

"What's the matter with the supper?" he asked.

"Nothing. I'm really not hungry."

"A nursing mother not hungry? That's strange. You look kind of peaked today too. Anything wrong?"

"No, nothing. Just not hungry." She did not want to tell him how sick she really was for fear she would be ordered back to bed. The household was getting back to order and she didn't want to jeopardize that.

She didn't get better. She began to throw up, even though she wasn't eating. She had no milk left for the baby, so she showed Elizabeth how to boil goat's milk, and fix it for feeding. Erna didn't like this change and screamed blue murder. It took awhile before hunger forced her to abandon her protest and accept the goat milk. With her tummy full and warm, her screaming stopped.

Two days later Katherine passed out while working in the kitchen. The children stared in shocked disbelief. Elizabeth put a cold rag on her forehead, telling the others to run and get dad and the midwife. When Katherine came to, Elizabeth helped her into bed. She felt helpless and fearful. What was wrong with her mother?

Husband and midwife arrived nearly at the same time. The midwife examined Katherine and her face blanched white.

"You better get a doctor fast," she advised.

"A doctor? But that could take days."

"I can't help her. She needs a doctor."

"But why? What's wrong?"

"She has an infection. I would say it has already spread further than it should have. I have nothing I can give her," she said, desperation in her voice.

"Nothing at all? Isn't there anything at all we can do?" Jochan was beginning to panic as reality struck him. He felt helpless. The urgency of the situation seemed like a bad dream.

"All I can say is keep sponging her with cold water. Try and keep the fever down and see if you can get liquids into her until a doctor can be brought. She needs medication that only a doctor would have."

"Will you stay and help?"

"Sure I will." The midwife was relieved, yet fearful. Would the family blame her if Katherine dies? She knew how fast infections spread, and she had little hope for Katherine.

The family tried unsuccessfully to locate a doctor. A few days before Christmas according to the Julian calendar and exactly ten days after the birth of Erna, Katherine died of milk fever. The initial joy the new baby brought suddenly turned to grief.

The family mourned.

The whole community, or village, mourned.

The baby cried night and day, as if she too was mourning the loss of her mother. The terrible loss would have a lasting and profound affect on Erna's life.

One can imagine the extra hurt, heartbreak, and strain this would have put on the family, and the village as a whole. Christmas festive celebrations came to a complete halt and many prayers were said.

The village had no cemetery. Katherine's death was the first to occur since the establishment of the village. An emergency meeting of the major family leaders was called. A location for a cemetery had to be chosen immediately. A grieving assembly made the decision.

Everyone in the village came for the funeral. Katherine's passing was a loss, not only to her family, but to the entire village. Her grave was the first one in the village. The family now had the distinction of having the first birth and the first death in their new society. The highest joy and the highest grief, all in the space of two weeks.

Again the villagers assembled in Jochan's house. This time they brought carefully prepared meals, and offers of sympathy and help for the family. The burden of managing the house now fell on Elizabeth. During the day she was so busy she didn't have time to cry, to feel down, or even to feel sorry for herself. But as she collapsed into her bed late at night, her sobs came uncontrollably. She tried stuffing her hand in her mouth and covering her head with the feather pillow. Nothing worked. She stuffed the pillow in her mouth, anything so she wouldn't be heard. Through her mind ran the thoughts, the ideas of why? why? why? What had she done wrong? She had tried her very best.

"Lisa."

Had she heard her name being called? She stopped crying to listen.

"Lisa, can I come in?" It was her dad.

"Okay." She quickly rubbed her eyes dry.

"Are you crying?"

She hung her head, not answering.

Jochan sat on the edge of her bed and put his arms around her. She laid her head on his shoulder and her tears burst forth freely.

Softly Jochan patted her back while fighting back his own tears. "It will be all right Lisa, it will be all right." But he wasn't sure he believed his own words.

Lisa looked up at him. "Why, dad? why? What did I do wrong?"

"You did nothing wrong, honey. It's just one of those things that happen. Only God knows why. Your in charge now. You know that, don't you? You will be Erna's mother. We are all depending on you."

Her tears stopped. She had to get control of herself. Her dad needed her. She would now be in charge of the family. She was now Erna's mother! Those words, given to her by her dad, were to stay with her, to cling to her words, deeds, and actions in future days, to be a stronghold of comfort and strength for her, to help her through good and bad days.

She gave her dad a hug. "I'm fine dad. Don't worry. I'll take care of things."

"I know you will."

Quietly he slipped out of the room, leaving his exhausted daughter find solace in sleep. A feeling of peace came over her.

As the line of visitors offering assistance began to dwindle, the household took on a semblance of organization and routine. The younger children began to look to Elizabeth for instruction and care. The two boys older than Elizabeth, worked with their dad, out of sight and sound. A much needed relief for a young girl trying to take over a large household.

The baby was becoming used to goat's milk and would snuggle down tight in Elizabeth's arms for her feedings. Erna was accepting Elizabeth as her new mother.

The new school was about to open. The building was complete and teachers were hired. Jochan announced that they would have to find someone to look after Erna during school hours. Elizabeth was heart broken. This was her baby, and she didn't want anyone else looking after her. Hadn't dad told her she was now the mother?

"Dad, I could quit school and stay home," she argued. "You need me here."

"Your education is more important," insisted Jochan. "No, you can't quit school."

"But I've got all the education I will probably ever use."

"Then chalk it up as a 'just in case' future safe guard."

"Please dad, Erna needs me."

"She will do quite all right while you're in school. We'll find someone good for her."

The other children, too, wanted Elizabeth to stay home. They were used to someone looking after them. They begged Jochan to let Elizabeth stay home. Feeling the extra responsibilities already bearing down on him, he finally agreed, but demanded in return:

"You must give her your full cooperation then."

"Oh, we will, we will," chorused the children.

The first morning of school brought total confusion.

No one seemed to know what to do on their own. Elizabeth had helped everyone make lunch the night before and was busy making breakfast for everyone when the problems began.

"Lisa, what should I wear?"

"Lisa, I can't find my socks."

"These pants need to be mended."

"Who has the comb? Lisa, I need to comb my hair."

It was in the middle of it all that Erna began to cry for her breakfast. Elizabeth immediately ran to attend to her.

"How come she gets the attention first?"

"Because she's a baby," replied Elizabeth.

"But she doesn't have to get to school on time."

"I know, but you guys can do for yourselves, she can't."

At this point Jochan and the two oldest boys came in for breakfast. They had been doing chores for several hours and were famished.

"Breakfast ready?"

At the sound of their father's voice everyone came running to him with their problems.

"And Lisa is just looking after the baby, and not us."

"Now, now! The baby comes first. You wouldn't want to eat your breakfast with her screaming and crying her little heart out, would you?"

Deftly Jochan took control, sending everyone scurrying on various duties while he finished his breakfast. Finally, with stomachs full, they all set about their day.

Slowly, but surely, the household became more and more efficient. But mother with her deft hands was never forgotten. The family did the best they could without her, but the one thing they could not fill in was the empty void in their father's life — the missing companionship of a woman's love and confidentiality. He desperately missed his wife of so many years.

When Erna was about a year old, Jochan shocked the family by bringing home a woman to introduce to them. Over supper he told the children of his plans to remarry. The children stared in disbelief. Somehow, out of politeness, they got through the meal without saying anything. But Jochan knew his family well. He knew that the silence meant trouble, but he wasn't about to change his mind. It was his life and his farm.

That night, one by one, the younger children tip-toed into Elizabeth's room. They were looking for comfort and hoping that Elizabeth would be able to change the situation.

"Do you think dad really will marry her?"

"I don't know, honey."

"She doesn't even look at all like mom. Mom was tiny and nice, she's huge and — and, she looks funny!"

"Yeah, she dresses funny, and her hair is funny."

"And she talks so loud."

"She's just different, that's all." Elizabeth tried to soothe them, but deep inside her resentment made her glad of their remarks. She was running things now. She didn't want anyone else coming in to take over, least of all a new step-mother! It was a long time before sleep came to the family that night.

Over the next few weeks the new lady was a constant visitor. She had been married before and had three nearly grown-up daughters. At first she tried her best to help around the house and win the children over, but it just didn't work. The two older boys ignored her, unless she spoke directly to them. What ever she went to do, Elizabeth would rush over with an, "I can do it. You don't have to."

This was especially true where Erna was concerned. No way was this woman going to get her hands on Lisa's baby! Being a year old, and very active, Erna loved people. Everyone was her friend, so she would eagerly respond to the woman's attention. Elizabeth had her hands full trying to keep them apart. Moreover Elsa, the next youngest, was four years old and loved attention too. She too welcomed the affections of the newcomer.

The three boys and one girl, ranging in age between Elizabeth and Elsa, took their cues from Elizabeth. If they were home from school, as soon as this new mother-to-be arrived, they would hastily whisk the girls off to play. The woman finally gave up. She determined to change the situation after she was married into the family. Then authority would be hers.

Jochan was not happy with the situation. He sat the children down and tried to reason with his children. But they responded negatively, especially Elizabeth who argued: "Why do we need someone else here dad? Aren't we doing good enough?"

"Yes, your doing just great. You don't need anyone, but I do."

"But why? We're all helping," said one of the younger boys.

"Well, it's hard to explain. A man just needs a woman."

"You just figure you need someone to sleep with," retorted Elizabeth angrily.

"Lisa! That 's enough!"

As the bitter tears began to flow, Elizabeth fled the room. Then, one by one, the boys filed out, not saying a word.

It was a quiet wedding. The only ones present were those who had to be. The village was well aware of the children's feelings. They themselves were divided on the issue. Some favored the children, others the father. Some had no opinion, or if they did, they kept it to themselves.

The woman moved in with piles of her belongings. Room had to be made for her furniture, her dishes, etc. Jochan sold some of the family belongings to make room for hers. Things did not go well. Everyone seemed upset and on edge, including Erna and Elsa, who always seemed to be in the way. Most certainly they were lacking the attention they usually got. They could not understand why Elizabeth ignored them, and then would suddenly grab them and hold them tight, so tight they could hardly breath as if she anticipated losing them and had to hang onto them with all her strength.

This new pair of hands began, immediately, to take control. This was now her house and she would run it her way! She deliberately belittled anything Elizabeth did. She changed things around for no other reason than to exert authority. The only thing in favor of the family was that her three daughters were on their own and did not move in too.

Elizabeth protested and quarreled with her. "But this is the way we've always done it. The children are used to it this way."

"Well not anymore. Things are going to be done my way and they will have to get used to it."

Elizabeth would then use her father as a means to try and win the conflict.

"But dad likes it this way."

"I'm sure he'll like my way as well."

Elizabeth would end up in tears, fleeing to her room to hide her anguish. She complained to her dad, only to have her concerns rejected.

"Well you know Lisa, she is in charge now. I trust you will try to make the necessary adjustments. It should be much easier for you, having someone to help with the work."

"But dad, she doesn't do things right. She purposely changes things just to make me mad."

"Oh, come on now Lisa, aren't you stretching things just a little?"

"No I'm not. She does, dad."

The two older boys supported Lisa's contentions. They did the best they could to help Elizabeth, without creating conflict. But Jochan did nothing. He didn't want to be caught between his new wife and his loving daughter. He was distressed and dismayed, but he hoped that everything would work its way out in time. Now he could see that this was not likely to happen.

Elizabeth had a boyfriend named Otto. His visits had not been very serious, but now, with Elizabeth so unhappy, things began to change. Otto became a frequent visitor who comforted her and listened sympathetically to her complaints.

He was a farmer, and had his own place. He was also an avid hunter. He had three beautiful hunting dogs. They were huge with long legs. The lead dog was entirely white, one was red and white, and the other was black and white. He bagged a lot of rabbits. Sometimes would go out early in the morning and come home with a rabbit before the days farming duties began. He was considered a dashing and stylish young man, envied by some for his sportsmanship and undaunted qualities of life.

Meat was scarce in Russia and many rabbits were eaten. They were not like our rabbits in Canada. They were much bigger and a different shade of brown.

Besides hunting rabbits, Otto liked to hunt red fox. The furs brought him a good income as red fox fur was very valuable. Since foxes killed many chickens, no one minded that they were hunted. Otto was thoroughly encouraged in all his escapades. Everyone thought that Elizabeth and he made a fine young couple.

Otto was now beginning to think that he really needed a wife to help him on the farm. Elizabeth was his ideal and he was very much in love with her. He believed the time was right to approach her on the subject. Before her step-mother moved in Elizabeth would not have dreamed of leaving her family. Now things were different.

Having made his decision, his next move was to try and get her far enough away from the rest of the family to ask for her hand. This took some doing since there was always someone around. The kids all liked him and eagerly followed him around whenever he came to visit. Then too, the dogs would usually show up with him. Everyone loved his graceful hunting dogs.

But, being an enterprising young man, he did of course, achieve his goal.

In a quiet moment, he said, "Lisa, I think you and I should get married. I sure could use a wife."

Somewhat surprised she replied, "But my family needs me."

"I need you more. Besides your dad is now remarried. He has someone to look after everything for him."

"But the kids — what would the kids do?"

"They'll manage just fine. They don't live far away. You could still look into things and help them. You're so unhappy here, you really need to leave. Besides, Lisa, I love you."

That was too much for Elizabeth. With tears coming to her eyes she threw her arms around him and said yes. They agreed to get married right away.

The family was delighted. They cheered, and congratulated the happy couple. Erna joined in with the joyous group, jumping up and down and clapping her little hands, not knowing what it would mean for her.

That night Elizabeth again had little visitors sneaking quietly into her room.

"Lisa, what about us?"

"What do you mean, what about you?"

"Well, when you get married, can we go with you?"

Elizabeth felt as if her heart were being torn out of her. "But dad needs you guys here."

"No he doesn't. He doesn't need us."

"But your his kids. He wouldn't let you go with me. And anyway, I won't be very far away. I can see you all the time."

"But it just won't be the same."

Elizabeth put her arms around them. "I know it won't, but I think you know I can't stay here any longer. You guys are all good workers and very smart. Everything will turn out just fine for you."

With their apprehensions calmed, they returned to their rooms. Elizabeth, unable to sleep, went to Erna's room and picked her up. There she sat, for most of the night, rocking her and holding her tight, her eyes never leaving her baby's face.

Chapter 2
Murder

The wedding was simple, but well planned. Jochan's new wife threw herself wholeheartedly into the preparations. After all, this would put an end to her biggest problem, or so she thought. She and Elizabeth almost became friends, during this time, with her allowing Elizabeth to make all the important decisions and then assisting to see that they were done. Closest family and friends attended. It was a happy time.

There was no honey moon. These were hard-working, conscientious people, and such extravagance would have been considered frivolous. There was just too much to be done on the farms for anyone to be able to leave them. So Elizabeth's honey moon was spent in her new home.

She was so busy, for the first two weeks, that she nearly forgot about her family. She didn't have time to think about them and worry about them. The kids had been instructed by their dad that they were not to go see Elizabeth for two weeks. She was to be left alone to get settled in her new home. This, of course, suited the step-mother just fine. It would give her time to make the transitions she felt were necessary.

But as soon as the two weeks were up, all of the younger children, except Erna and Elsa who were too young, dropped in on Elizabeth. Elizabeth was overjoyed and hastily arranged a tea party. She listened to all their complaints, fears, and troubles and offered all the advise she could.

"And Lisa?"

"Yeah?"

"Erna misses you so much."

"Yeah! She cries a lot and looks so sad. She keeps asking for you and looking for you."

Elizabeth felt terrible. The very next day she went back home to check on things herself. Erna came running to her, threw her arms around her, and clung for dear life. Elizabeth held her tight, tears coming to her eyes.

When Elizabeth had to leave, her step-mother tried to take Erna from her. Erna resisted. She was kicking and screaming when Jochan entered. Gently he took Erna from Elizabeth who then left with the baby's heart breaking cries, "Li—a, Li—a," ringing in her ears.

Elizabeth cried all the way back home. How could she have been so selfish as to leave her baby for her own interests? What kind of a person was she? Then slowly, a plan began to form. She stopped crying. Why it was a wonderful plan! Why hadn't she thought of it before? She could hardly wait for Otto to get home so she could tell him. She was certain he would agree to it.

Otto was not so certain. He was a very kind hearted man and would do anything for Elizabeth, but he was not sure her dad would agree to her plan.

This stopped Elizabeth short. What if her dad didn't agree? But he just had to! She was sure she could convince him that it was the best for all concerned.

Elizabeth couldn't wait. The next evening she and Otto went over to talk to her dad privately.

Greeting them with a smile, he said. "So, what is this very important, secret that is so urgent?"

"Dad," Elizabeth swallowed hard, "we want to adopt Erna."

His mouth fell open. He stared hard at her. "You what?"

She found herself getting uncomfortable. "We want to adopt Erna."

"Are you out of your mind?"

Elizabeth shriveled inside. "But she needs me dad. I'd take good care of her. You said she was my baby."

"When I said she was your baby I meant for you to look after as long as was needed. She's my child and she now has a mother to care for her."

"But she wants to be with me." Elizabeth was trying not to sob.

"She'll get over it."

Otto tried to stick up for Elizabeth, saying it would be good for the baby and for them, that she would have an excellent home and wouldn't be very far away. The more they talked the angrier dad got.

He finally jumped to his feet shouting, "absolutely not, and that's final! She's my child and she will stay here! This meeting is over! I've never heard of anything so silly."

Otto put his arm around Elizabeth's shaking body and helped her out. As they were going out the door her dad demanded, "...and nothing of this will be spoken to anyone. I expect the same of you. I don't want anyone hurt."

Elizabeth wondered what he meant by that. They were the ones being hurt. And so was Erna, having to be looked after by that woman! But what about the rest of the younger ones? Could her dad mean that they would be hurt, thinking maybe she was playing favorites? And was she playing favorites? It suddenly dawned on her that maybe she was. But she was only trying to do right where the greatest need was, wasn't she? Besides Erna was her baby. Her dad had said so and what ever he said could not be erased now.

Elizabeth visited the girls as much as she dared, without incurring the wrath of her step-mother. The rest of the children spent as much time as they dared at Elizabeth's home. Even with Elizabeth out of the way, things did not go as peacefully as they should have in her father's home. It just seemed that this new mother would not be accepted as she should have been.

The tense atmosphere made the oldest boy decide to leave home and start his own place. Reluctantly dad agreed to help him. It was dad who would miss him the most. This left the next two older boys to do more work, so they were unable to spend as much time with Elizabeth and Otto as before. They did feel more grown up now that they were able to do that which they were not allowed to do before, and to be able to help their dad in making a living. Best of all, they got to stay home from school when help was most needed.

Over the next three years, not only did the oldest boy start up his own farm, but two babies were born into the family. The first was a girl, born to their step-mother, the other a boy, born to Elizabeth. Both babies were healthy and active, keeping their mothers very busy.

This was great for the new mothers. It took their minds off of their differences and disagreements. It was not so great for Erna and Elsa, who now found themselves lacking attention from both sides. Bill, the third boy, and next oldest after Elizabeth, found himself, not only assisting his dad more, but attending to the two smaller girls. He took them almost everywhere he went. Everyone loved the girls and showered them with hugs and treats.

At this time the village experienced a smallpox epidemic. No one had been vaccinated, indeed vaccination was mostly unheard of and unavailable in the village.

"Smallpox! smallpox! smallpox!" The cry echoed throughout the settlement, as house after house displayed the dreaded quarantine signs on their doors. Visiting and business slowed to a near halt. Only those activities necessary to maintain life were carried on.

Erna, now four-years-old, had been crying a lot lately. Bill examined her and found her very hot.

"Dad, Erna's sick." said Bill.

Dad hurried to Erna's side. His face turned pale when he felt her forehead. Quickly, he assembled the household together.

"I think Erna has the smallpox," he told his solemn family. She will have to be kept in her room alone. No one is to go in. Bill, we're going to put you in charge of nursing her. We'll tell you exactly what to do and how to do it."

"But why me?" asked Bill.

"Because you have been with her the most lately. There is a good possibility that you are already infected. We will need a quarantine sign on our door. No more going any place or seeing anyone until this is all over."

"Will Erna die?" asked one of the children.

"We will pray that she doesn't," answered Dad.

"Can't we go see Lisa?" asked another.

"No you can't!" answered Dad curtly.

Erna suffered the classic viral symptoms of smallpox: high fever, skin eruptions, itching and pain.

As disinfectants, soaps, hot water, cold water, towels, rags, special bedding, etc., was collected and put into use, the family gradually came to the stunning realization of the seriousness of the situation. If the disease spread to the rest of the family, they could all die! Some, in the village, were already gone.

Erna sobbed continuously, tossing and turning, unable to sleep much day or night. Bill did his very best. He sponged her with cold water to bring down the fever. He forced her to drink as much liquid as he could. He held her and comforted her. She clung tightly to him and sometimes called for Lisa. Bill got so tried that he found himself crying and falling asleep sitting up.

Then the fever started to subside and a rash began to appear. Erna had made it through the first round. Everyone began to have hope. As the rash got worse pimples began to appear. Erna started to scratch and Bill could not stop her. Finally, in desperation, he wrapped rags around her hands, but she managed to tear the rags off. Bill put them back on, wrapping them all the way up the arm and tying them at the shoulders.

The cold water sponging was replaced with warm soda water sponging, to try to stop the itching.

Then Bill came down with the disease. His step-mother found Erna sleeping peacefully and Bill sitting beside her in a chair. He was hot and delirious. Horrified, she sent one of the children after their dad. He arrived quickly.

Dad turned the farming operation over to John, the second son and the oldest one home. The operation included three or four hired men. To further complicate the situation, they were in the middle of training a bunch of oxen for sale. He told John to do the best he could, he was going to nurse Bill himself. Perhaps he was feeling guilty over making Bill nurse Erna. Was Bill infected before, or did he contact it from Erna? It is very likely that he got it from Erna as she was now nearly well and he should have gotten it sooner if he had already been infected.

Using all the knowledge he had on containing infectious diseases, their dad carefully and meticulously took care of Bill. He also looked after Erna, who, still not very active, was not allowed to join the rest of the family. The long hours of worry and lack of sleep began to take their toll on him and he would find himself dozing in spite of all efforts to stay awake. When this happened Erna would sneak out of the room. They finally decided she was probably past the infectious stages anyway, and let her join the rest of the family. This made things somewhat easier for Jochan.

Time after time he brought Bill back to reality by calling his name, talking to him, assuring him that he was there and taking care of him. Slowly Bill began to recover. The family was jubilant. Two people, in their family, had survived the dreaded disease. Many friends and neighbours had not. This was heart breaking to them, in spite of their happiness over their own good fortune. Nervously they watched each other for signs of someone else getting smallpox. As each day passed and no one else did, they breathed easier.

Soon Bill was out of isolation and the quarantine sign came down. Every square inch of the isolation room was disinfected, plus everything in it. Things that couldn't be disinfected were burned. Moreover, the room was left vacant for a long time before being used again. They had a large house and there was no desperate need for the room. In the village the disease gradually subsided and things began to get back to normal.

What could never be returned to normal were Erna's and Bill's faces. The pockmarks were forever be a reminder of the grief and sorrow the terrible disease caused. In later years Erna's children did not know what caused their mother's marked facial features. To them she just had a unique quality of skin, which only added to her beauty.

As Bill's health improved, he and his dad were drawn closer together from all they had been through. Jochan began to rely on Bill to help train the oxen. That is why Bill got to go to the city with Jochan to sell the oxen. Bill delighted in his special privilege and thoroughly enjoyed an exciting day. Two of the hired men also went to help with the oxen. John stayed behind, manning the home front.

The day progressed well. They had gotten the oxen loaded and made the trip to the big city without any mishaps. There all the oxen were sold for top price. Their dad had received thousands of rubles cash for them.

Breathing a big sigh of relief dad said, "Well men, good job done, let's go get a room for the night. I could use some nourishment and rest."

They got two rooms, one for Bill and his dad and one for the two hired men. By the time they finished eating, it was already getting late. Bill and his dad went up to their room, leaving the two hired men to their own diversions.

"You know son, I am exhausted. Think I'm going to call it a day and retire for the night."

"Dad?"

"Yeah?"

"Would you mind if I took in a movie before going to bed?"

"Well, I guess not. Don't very often get to the city so you'd have the chance to do such a thing. Sure, go ahead. Just bang on the door when you get back. I'll hear you and let you in."

He put the container of money under the bed and flopped down. Bill excitedly left, carefully locking the door behind him. The movie turned out to be a good one, at least Bill thought it was, but maybe that was because he very seldom got to go to one. It was late when he got back to the hotel, and he was tired. His footsteps were dragging as he pulled himself up the stairs to their room.

He knocked softly on the door. He didn't want to disturb other guests. He waited. No answer. He knocked a bit harder. Still no answer. Now he was getting somewhat annoyed with his dad. Surely the man wasn't that sound of a sleeper! He banged harder on the door and put his ear against it to listen. He could hear nothing. A flash of fear shot through him. What was wrong with his dad? In desperation he pounded as hard as he could.

"Stop that banging out there!" shouted a voice from the next room. "A body can't get any sleep in this place!"

Frantically Bill ran in search of the proprietor.

"My dad, my dad, something is wrong with my him, he doesn't answer!"

"Hold it son! Calm down!" said the proprietor, "I don't know what you're talking about."

Bill swallowed hard, trying to get control of himself. "My dad and I have a room here. I was at the theatre. He said to knock when I got back. There is no answer. I just know something has happened to him."

"Oh come on, he could just be sound asleep."

"Not as hard as I banged on the door."

"Okay. Let's go see."

Slowly, much too slowly for Bill, the manager went up to the room and opened the door.

The room was empty. The window had been smashed and there was glass everywhere. It looked like a struggle had taken place. Bedding and furniture were strewn around. Bill ran and looked under the bed. The container of money was gone. Then he spotted a chair in the corner with his dads clothing laid neatly across it. That meant his dad had left in his underwear!

"Look, my dad's clothes are still here. He had no other clothes with him!" Bill's horror showed in his voice.

The manager looked out of the broken window. It looked like someone had been forcibly dragged through the window and along the ground on the other side. He put an arm around Bill.

"Come on son. We're going to call the police."

After several hours, the police arrived. The remainder of the night was spent investigating, but to no avail. Dad could not be found. The two hired men were found sound asleep in their room. They cooperated the best they could. Bill's family were contacted and John arrived as quickly as he could. The two boys launched their own search, but could not find their dad.

Two days passed. Then, as the boys were about to have lunch, the police paid them a visit. Their father had been found in a lumber yard, in his underwear, with a big pole across his neck. He had been murdered. The motive? The pile of money, of course, as it was gone. Now, who knew about the money besides Bill? The two hired workers! They became the prime suspects, but proof could not be found. The men had air tight alibis supported by witnesses concerning their whereabouts during the time in question.

Proof was only found years later when one of the culprits lay dying. He called for a priest and confessed to the murder. He wanted the priest to pray for him, before he died. After his death the priest told the police of the confession. The family was then informed. The other man could not be found. Perhaps he too had died. This conclusion to the murder bitterly turned the family against the Catholic church. Their animosity was to be passed on to future generations of their progeny.

The boy's took their dad's body home. There was a large funeral with all those from the village, who still weren't battling small pox, attending. His body was laid to rest beside his first wife's. The children calmly, and with great dignity, took over all responsibility from their step-mother. It was very plain that sympathies were on the side of the children. They now considered themselves orphans, having neither a mother nor a dad.

Shortly after the funeral the family members met to settle legal matters. The solemn group would decide the future of their lives. Only Erna was unaware of the gravity of the situation, although even she knew that something very bad had happened—that things were, again not as they should be. Already she missed her dad and followed Bill around like a little shadow that didn't want to be lost.

There were several different men in charge of settling what had become a large estate. The first matter to be settled was the farm itself. Dating back from Biblical times, this would be inherited, as a birth right, by the eldest son. But in this case the eldest son had already taken his portion and left to start his own farm. The farm, therefore, was left to the second oldest son, John. Since John had already been in charge of much of the operation, he would have no problem carrying on. He would eliminate the hired help and run the operation on a smaller scale until he could build it back up. The main reason for the reduced size would be the lack of funds with which to operate as cash settlements were dealt out to other family members.

Their step-mother was to receive a large cash settlement, which the family considered to be too much. She would take her money and move back to where she had come from, taking the baby with her. The family were never to see her or their half-sister again. They did hear that she was married twice more after that.

After receiving her share, Elizabeth quietly addressed the group. "I have a request" she said. "Otto and I would like Erna to live with us. Considering the present circumstances, we feel it would be in every one's best interests."

No one spoke, everyone just sat looking at each other, waiting for the other person to say something. Their step-mother sat with her head hanging, eyes on the floor, she too said nothing. Elizabeth's hands shook, surely they couldn't deny her the right to her baby now.

Finally John spoke as the new head of the family. "You do have your own baby now. Do you really want two small ones?"

"Oh yes! Most certainly." Elizabeth's voice pleaded.

"Then I have no problem with it. In fact, I think it's an excellent idea."

Everyone agreed. Elizabeth smiled, her heart jumping with joy. "Thank you. Thank you so much." Running across the room she grabbed Erna and drew her close to her. Finally, she had her baby back. Erna snuggled down, safe and secure, in Elizabeth's arms. She seemed to know that this was where she belonged; this was her mother.

Reaching one little hand up she patted Elizabeth's face murmuring, "Lisa, Lisa."

So it was that in the midst of great sorrow, God brought unspeakable joy.

There was one provision, in the will, that surprised everyone, and not everyone was happy with it. Extra money was set aside for the youngest boy, Emil, for his schooling. People at that time paid to send their kids to school. There were no government funded schools, and private schools cost dearly. Why was Emil favored? Because he was very good in school. Still it did not seem right to some of the relatives. But the terms of the will could not be changed. John would administer the money and take care to see that his dad's wishes were carried out. Emil would have to board in the city to complete his schooling.

There had been another child named Emil. Before the family had established themselves in their new village, he had drowned in a large, deep pool of water in the back yard that the children used as a swimming pool. He was only two years old. Perhaps this had something to do with their dad's decision.

The child had been all dressed up, with a little white hat on. It was Sunday and he was waiting to go to church. When he was missed, the family ran for the pool. Floating on top of the water, was the little white hat. Some one dove into the water and brought him out, but it was too late. He was dead. When the next child was born, he was named Emil after his brother who drowned.

After all parts of the will had been thoroughly discussed, one last request was made by Jochan's sister. She requested that Elsa come live with her. She argued that Elsa was also too small not to have a mother to look after her. All agreed. That left Bill, Henry, Emil, and Alwina, the youngest, to stay on the farm with John.

The aunt had three girls of her own. She lived a great distance away, but would do her best to look in occasionally to see how everyone was doing. The family began to be split up and pulled apart as life took its course. Decisions were made and different paths were followed.

Erna took to her new home like a duck to water. She loved the baby and constantly wanted to help take care of him. Elizabeth quite enjoyed her new role as mother of two, after all she had been taking care of more than that before she got married. The only indication Erna gave of missing her old home was when she would wander about, once in awhile, asking, "Where Bill? Where Bill?"

Otto and Elizabeth both loved horses and had many. Russian winters are long and very cold. One of their favorite activities, was to harness the horses and take the children for sleigh rides. The hunting dogs would follow along, barking with happiness. Wolves were very numerous, in fact there were so many they would become increasingly short of prey, and so very hungry. Perhaps it was this that prompted them to follow after any moving object, including sleighs drawn by horses, or horse back riders.

The gray wolf was prominent in Russia at that time. Even though they are called gray wolves, their color can range from black to brown to gray to white. The average-sized adult male was three feet or more high at the shoulder and four feet or more long, not counting the tail. They weighed between one hundred and two hundred pounds. Some even more. They could run at speeds as high as thirty-five miles an hour and clear sixteen feet in a bound. While hunting, a speed of twenty miles an hour could be maintained for many hours. Horses were no match for them. They ran in packs, numbering as many as thirty to a pack.

Everyone carried rifles. Simply shooting into the air would cause the wolves to disperse. Being a hunter, Otto didn't just shoot into the air, and many a hapless wolf fell victim to others in the pack when it fell, or became wounded from Otto's rifle. Neighbors encouraged him to hunt the wolves because of their raids on livestock, including his own. Also, there were stories that both horses and riders, plus horse drawn vehicles had, in fact, been attacked by the wolves.

In Otto and Elizabeth's case his marksmanship prevented any such attacks. They did, however, have one big problem—the hunting dogs. They were large, but not as large as some of the wolves.

The presence of wolves was enough to drive them crazy, and, even though they were well trained, it was difficult to keep them from chasing after the wolves.

One early spring day, when the family was on an outing, a small wolf suddenly appeared out of the brush a few yards from the sleigh. This was too much for the dogs. Barking furiously they lunged to the attack. Frightened, the horses bolted, jerking the sleigh behind them.

"Grab the kids Lisa. We'll have things under control here in a minute."

Otto needn't have warned Elizabeth. She already had hold of her babies, clutching them tightly.

"Whoa there girls, easy up, easy now."

With experienced hands Otto brought the horses under control. He then turned them around in the direction from which they had come.

"Why are we going back?"

"Can't leave the dogs."

"They'll come."

"Might be more wolves around."

Elizabeth shuttered. "What are you going to do?"

"Bring them back."

As they approached the area where the wolf had been, they could hear the violent barking of the dogs off in the bush.

Grabbing his rifle, Otto handed the reins to Elizabeth. "Here. Hold the horses tight. I won't be long."

"Otto, I'm scared."

"Don't worry. I'll only be a few minutes."

Jumping down he took off through the bush in the direction of the barking dogs.

Erna crept slowly up to Elizabeth's side. "Can I help Lisa?"

"No honey, you just go hold tight to baby. He has to stay sitting. That will help me a lot."

"Okay Lisa."

They waited for what seemed like forever. Finally, just as Elizabeth was debating what to do, Otto walked out from behind the bushes. The dogs were jumping at his side. Elizabeth stared. He looked like he was carrying something besides his gun.

Erna was the first to realize what he had.

"Puppy, puppy," she screamed leaping up and pointing at Otto. The baby, following her lead, tried to get to his feet. Elizabeth was having a hard time keeping the horses in line. Suddenly it dawned on her what he really had—a wolf cub! No wonder the horses wouldn't stay still; they could smell it. So could the dogs. That's why they were acting so queer.

Quickly Otto swung himself up on the sleigh.

"The dogs killed its mother. I just couldn't leave it there to die."

"Was there only one?" Elizabeth eyed the little animal with apprehension.

"All I could find. She either just had one or something happened to the others."

"Puppy, puppy," Erna crawled over to pet the cub. It did not appreciate the attention. Otto held its head and paws in such a manner that it could not harm the children as they pet it. Elizabeth was still too busy trying to handle the horses. The dogs were bouncing up and down beside the sleigh.

So it was that the baby wolf had a new home. A special pen had to be build for it to keep the dogs away or they would have ripped it apart. The dogs never did become friendly with it, and many a growling session occurred between them. Nor did the wolf ever become people friendly. Elizabeth and Otto found themselves constantly feeling fear around it and, because of their fear, having to fight to keep the kids away from it.

One day, as it grew up, it somehow climbed up and over the pen escaping back into the wild where it belonged. Even the dogs did not realize it had gone as they issued no warning, or perhaps they were just glad to see the last of it.

It was during this time that John got married. This, again, changed the situation of the home farm. A new pair of hands would be in charge of running the household. Perhaps this was part of the reason that Bill approached his brother John.

"You know, John, I think I'll write uncle Oscar in the United States and see if I can go there and work for him."

"You what?" John nearly fell off his chair.

Bill was embarrassed. "Think I'll see if I can get into the U.S. Start a different life, you know."

"But why? I need your help here. You must realize that."

"Yeah, I know. Just think this face needs a climate change."

"Nothing wrong with your face." It was now John's turn to be embarrassed.

"Maybe in your opinion, but these pock marks are giving me an inferior complex. I need to go where no one knows me."

"But where ever you go, people will get to know you."

"Sure, but it will be different. They won't know how I looked before."

"Well, it's entirely up to you. Sure hate to see you go though."

Bill did write uncle Oscar (he was an uncle on his mother's side of the family), and he did get permission to enter the United States in the care of his uncle in North Dakota.

Saying goodbye to family, friends, and his girlfriend was very hard. They could not understand why he wanted to go. Perhaps he was not all together certain himself, especially when the final goodbye time arrived. Tears flowed freely and nearly caused Bill to change his mind at the last minute. Erna clung tightly to him, seeming to realize that it would be years before she would ever see him again.

Bill worked a couple of years for his uncle and then enlisted in the United States army under President Theodore Roosevelt. World War I was about to begin. Because Bill was a good soldier, he was promoted and later chosen to train young army cadets for the war. He felt he had made the right choice in coming to the United States, and loved his new country dearly.

After the war Bill received a substantial army pension. While visiting relatives in Canada, he got married, at which time Erna got to see him again. It was a happy reunion.

Bill died of cancer in August of 1963. Erna was able to visit with him once in awhile during his last years. His wife died in 1994, at the age of 91.

Chapter 3

Noah's Ark

World War I started in 1914. Erna was six years old and just beginning school. The Russian Revolution began in 1917, and lasted until 1923. Prior to these chaotic events, the family home was a beautiful estate. A large flower garden was situated on the left as you entered the driveway followed by a vegetable garden and an orchard containing a variety of fruit trees. Further on loomed a grand house with spacious rooms. All had hardwood floors, except the extra large, maroon kitchen-dining room which had a brick floor. The brick helped keep the kitchen cool during hot weather.

There was a large basement. The ceiling and top half of the sides were finished with brick. The bottom half of the sides and the floor were earthen. Here potatoes and vegetables were stored. One side of the basement contained wooden stands on which wooden barrels stood about two feet off the floor. These barrels held grape juice. About twelve brick steps led from one end of the basement to a little lobby with double doors opening onto a driveway where horse-pulled wagons parked to unload food and supplies. A small side door led to the kitchen.

A huge mulberry tree stood in front of the house. Some of its branches led up to the roof. Erna would often climb the tree and then shinny along a limb to the roof. From this vantage point she would find the biggest mulberries to pick. This pleased Elizabeth, until she discovered what Erna was doing to get these wonderful mulberries.

"These are beautiful berries, Erna," said Elizabeth one day when Erna presented her with an extra large quantity of the lush berries. "How do you find them? I can never find any that big."

Erna bowed her head and said nothing.

"Well, come on, share your secret, persisted Elizabeth."

"I get them from higher up."

"How do you do that?"

"I just climb a little bit."

"And how little is a little bit, Erna?"

"Up onto the branches."

"Like maybe up onto the roof of the house?"

No answer.

"Yes, Erna?"

Erna nodded.

"Look, I don't want you climbing up there anymore. You could fall and get hurt, understand?"

Again Erna nodded. But there were times that the temptation to climb that tree was more than Erna could bear.

Opposite the main house stood a small summer house. It also had a large kitchen where the women did the canning, and baking. It had bedrooms in the back for the hired help. Next to the summer house stood a flour mill run by a big steam engine. A line of other buildings followed. They were constructed with galvanized joining roofs in a way that rain water could be collected and directed to an underground well. The residents always enjoyed ice cold drinking water from that well. Watermelons were grown in abundance and frequently lowered, by bucket, down the well to keep cold.

Emil was now attending school in the city. He came home on weekends and holidays. He asked John if he could stay in the attic when he was home. John agreed and Emil remodeled it to resemble an apartment. He had his own bedroom, a small eating room, a sitting room, and a special room for drawing and painting. He loved art and Erna can remember taking some of his work to school for 'show and tell.'

Emil also loved birds and animals. He saved one side of the attic for pigeons. An opening allowed the pigeons to fly in and out and nest inside. He had names for many of them, and seemed to know them all. They would come when he called, eat out of his hands, and sit on his shoulders. They multiplied in abundance. Even so, it seemed to Emil that, now and then, some went missing. He decided to investigate. He first approached John and asked him if he had seen any dead pigeons around lately.

"Dead pigeons?" repeated John with surprise.

"Yeah, I seem to be missing some."

"How can you know you're missing some when you have so many?"

"Well, I'm just positive that some of the younger ones are gone."

"Maybe they migrated to some of the neighbours."

"Possible, but I doubt it. They get fed too well here."

"That's for sure!" said Alwina who, along with John's wife, now ran the household. John's wife was busy at the stove and never turned around.

Emil suspiciously stared at the two women. He turned to Henry. "What about you, Henry?"

"What about me?"

"Have you seen any of my pigeons lying around?"

"Nope. Haven't seen any lying around any place."

"Alwina?"

"What?"

"Do you know anything about them?"

"I think you better go count your pigeons again."

More questioning got Emil no where. He felt like he was getting 'the run around.' They all knew what happened to the pigeons and no one wanted to tell him. He was sure of that. It was also obvious that Alwina thought he had too many pigeons. He was determined to get to the bottom of it. If anyone would be straight forward it would be Erna. He could find out from her.

With this in mind, he paid Elizabeth and Otto a visit. When he left, he took Erna with him to his attic apartment, where he entertained Erna by playing the guitar and singing songs he himself made up. Some of these he taught Erna. Soon he and Erna were busy singing their favorite songs. Feeling down about his pigeons, he made up a new song for her entitled, "The Bird With The Broken Wing."

Erna didn't know anything about the pigeons. She didn't know any were missing. She felt bad, for Emil and for the pigeons, and said she would see if she could find out what was happening to them. She was not to find out until a few years later, when it was too late to inform Emil. It seems, meat being scarce, Alwina had been catching the pigeons and cooking them. They made good pigeon meat pies. Emil probably guessed that this was what was happening.

Before Erna was taken home, Emil fed her his own special treat—dill pickles dipped in syrup. Years later Erna would claim that this was the reason she liked sweet and sour cuisine so much. Erna adored Emil and spent many happy hours with him in his attic apartment while he was a student.

Everyone liked Emil and considered him to be a gentleman and a scholar. The only person who didn't seem to care for Emil was John's wife. She seemed to be unhappy about the extra money that was left him for school. Her idea was that a young healthy man like Emil should be out working in the fields and on the farm, not going to school.

At this time rumors of war began to circulate. Rivalry between the great European powers came to a head with the assassination of Archduke Francis Ferdinand of Austria-Hungary by a Serbian nationalist on June 28, 1914. Austria-Hungary, supported by Germany, declared war on Serbia. Russia went to Serbia's defense and was soon joined by Great Britain, France, Belgium, Montenegro, and Japan. The Ottoman Empire joined Germany and Austria-Hungary.

News of war spread like wild fire throughout the village. Russia was now at war, and against Germany. How would that affect the many Germans living in Russia? It was their home and they fully supported Russia. But would Russian officials understand that? Fear and worry invaded the minds of every German resident old enough to understand what was happening. Stores became empty as the necessities of life were purchased and hoarded in anticipation of shortages.

Otto, being of Russian descent, was the first to be called to go to war. A Russian Cossack arrived on horseback at his door and handed him a piece of paper. Saluting smartly, he wheeled his horse and was gone. Otto read the paper and walked slowly into the house. His face told the story, as he looked at Elizabeth.

"You've been called to go," said Elizabeth, horror in her eyes.

"I'm afraid so."

"Oh Otto!" She threw her arms around him in dismay. "What if something happens to you?"

"Nothing will happen to me. I'll be okay."

"What's wrong Lisa?" inquired Erna as she approached Lisa.

"It's going to be all right Erna," said Elizabeth. "Otto has just been called to go fight in the war for our country." She put her arms around Erna to soothe her, but Erna could tell by her voice that everything wasn't okay, and she was afraid.

Erna looked up at Otto. "What will we do without you?"

Elizabeth was thinking the same thing as tears appeared in her eyes.

Otto did his best to act nonchalant, but inside he felt sick and worried. We'll just have to get one of your big brothers over here to help Elizabeth until I get back home.

"How long will you be gone?" asked Erna.

"I don't know, honey, I don't know."

Otto was given only two days to make arrangements; then he was gone.

In August of 1914, Russia invaded East Prussia, but was decisively defeated. By the autumn of 1915, combined Austro-German efforts had driven Russia out of most of Poland, and Russia was scrambling to acquire more man power. Both Henry and Emil were called up and ordered to go at once. The two oldest brothers were left to take care of the farms. With most of the men gone, the women were left to work in the fields which they found very difficult.

Farmers were being asked to sell their livestock to help feed the army. The family would have had to do this any way, because they didn't have enough help to look after them. Erna, at age six, took over the duties of cook, house cleaner, and child care worker. She missed many days of school. Because of defeats on the battlefield, corruption in government, and overwhelming hardships, people in Russia became increasingly discontent with the government and the war.

In 1916 Russia counterattacked in a powerful drive to retake what they had lost. However, by the end of the year the offensive had collapsed and had cost Russia many thousands of lives. It was then that Henry was discharged from the army and returned home. His body, from fighting and standing in swamps, had given out. He suffered with arthritis so bad, he could hardly move. He looked twenty years older and weighed very little.

Everyone was shocked as he put his head down on the table and began to cry. Great wracking sobs shook his dilapidated body.

"It's just unreal out there! You just wouldn't believe it, men dying all around you, the stench, screams ... we were unable to rescue many of the wounded. We just left them for the German army. Not enough to eat ... they couldn't get the food to us. Some of our men begged to die—to be shot rather than left. Seen one guy do it too! Can't say I blame him."

Henry talked on and on. It seemed that telling it was a release to him, like he was shedding a bad dream.

"Have you seen Otto or Emil?"

"No. We weren't together at all. Don't know anything that's happened to them."

Good care and good food soon slowly put Henry back on his feet and he began to work with John on the home farm.

The summer of 1916 was extremely hot, which adding to the difficulties of trying to keep the farms going without enough workers. Erna was now eight and in grade three at school.

Just before school let out for the summer she came home tremendously excited.

"Lisa, Lisa, guess what?"

"What?"

"They're saying at school that Noah's Ark has been seen on Mount Ararat."

"Don't be silly Erna. It hasn't been seen for years. Why would it all of a sudden appear now?"

Elizabeth knew the ark was up there. They were taught all about it at school and considered themselves very special to be living as close as they were to that wonderful mountain of the Bible.

"But it's true, Lisa, it's true. They say because it is so hot the snow and ice have melted enough to be able to see it. Can we go see the ark Lisa? Can we?"

"Even if it's true, Erna, there's no way we could go see it. It would be too dangerous, and who would take care of things here? We can't climb that mountain!"

"But we wouldn't have to, we could just see it from a distance."

"Just forget it Erna."

Erna walked away with downcast eyes. She so desperately wanted to see the ark. Maybe if she prayed real hard, God would allow her to see it.

The next day Henry came by to help on the farm. He verified Erna's information. Yes, everyone was talking about it. Erna jumped up and down with joy. Elizabeth found her heart beating fast. What if they should be able to see it?

A few days later, as if in answer to Erna's prayers, an extra ordinary weather phenomenon occurred that made the mountains appear closer than they really were. Early that morning Erna stepped outside and was struck with awe. There appeared on Mount Ararat a tiny black dot about three quarters of the way up. She knew it was Noah's Ark. Erna, in later years, recalled the dot as being near the center, on a high peak. Since they lived north of Mount Ararat, this would put the ark on the north side of the mountain. Research verified that the ark was seen by Russians in the army during this time.

Erna thanked God for answering her prayers, then ran to Elizabeth.

"Lisa, Lisa, come quickly! the ark! you can see the ark!"

"Erna, your being silly again," replied Elizabeth. Can't you see how busy I am?"

"No, no! Really Lisa, it's true, please come look!"

Elizabeth decided to humor her. But then she too saw the inspiring sight. She could hardly believe her eyes! Grabbing the children they ran all the way to the home farm to inform the rest of the family. They had a telescope through which the ark could be viewed with greater clarity. The dark dot became more like a brown square.

In reverent solemnity the family gathered together in the house for prayers. The oldest son, Jacob, and his family had also been called in. John was the first to speak.

"You know, I think we should go up there." He looked at the women. "Think you gals could hold out here for a week while we take a closer look?"

The women looked wearily at each other. They were already short handed and summer work was falling behind, but could such an opportunity be passed by?

Alwina said, "Sure, we'll manage. You go ahead."

Erna was jumping around the table like a jack rabbit.

"Erna, save your energy for work. Your going to get lots of it."

"You know," said Jacob, "what we need is to hire a plane and zoom down for some close-up pictures."

John agreed. "Excellent idea, but where do we get a plane now? There's a war on you know."

Henry had friends who had a plane. They would be interested in such a venture.

So it was that a plane, plus two more men, was obtained. With all the military action taking place, the plane was not noticed, or so they thought, as it flew around the mountain taking pictures of the area that the men thought accessible for climbing, plus close-up pictures of the ark, sticking out of an ice glacier.

With the pictures developed, the family again gathered together with the families of the two men. The pictures were passed around and viewed with fascination.

The men decided to climb the mountain and examine the ark. They bought the necessary equipment for the climb and within a few days everything was organized for the expedition. Their one regret was that Otto, Bill, and Emil could not be with them. How they would have loved this undertaking.

Then disaster struck. A group of Bolsheviks on horseback approached the house. The Bolsheviks were against the war and refused to take part in it. More and more people flocked to their side as the war caused greater and greater hardships to everyone.

John and Henry walked out to meet them.

"Can we help you?" John asked.

"Yeah," the leader of the group answered. "You can hand over that climbing equipment you purchased."

"Why, is there something wrong with it?"

"No, nothing wrong with it, just with the purpose you were going to use it for."

"What do you mean? We're using it for mountain climbing. That's what it's made for."

"Sure, for climbing that Mount Ararat with, well that's restricted territory. You can't go there."

"Since when?"

"Since we said so." At his words the rest of the men circled John and Henry.

A chill ran down John's spine, but he wasn't going to give up all their expensive equipment without a fight. Henry said nothing. Memories of the war struck fear in him.

"What authority do you have to say so?"

"The authority of this." The men aimed their guns at John and Henry. They had no choice but to turn over their equipment. Still the Bolsheviks were not satisfied.

"We want the photos too, plus negatives," demanded the leader.

"What photos?"

"Don't act ignorant man. The ones you took of the mountain. All of them!"

With sinking hearts they gave up the pictures and negatives. Then the Bolsheviks helped themselves to a few chickens and left.

The family felt devastated. Erna couldn't stop crying.

"We need to report them Lisa, okay Lisa? We need to make them give us back our things."

Elizabeth agreed, but in her heart she knew they couldn't. They were fighting against Germany. Who would listen to the complaints of Germans in this country? No one. She was sure of that! In fact, they would probably get in worse trouble by putting in a complaint.

This event marked the beginning of all their troubles. They came under constant surveillance.

Years later Erna insisted that she knows the ark is still exactly where she saw it, in spite of what anyone else might believe or say, and that when God wants the world to see it, it will be there for all to see, preserved and intact.

Shortly after the incident with the Bolsheviks, a regular army soldier stopped to see Elizabeth. Fearfully, she went out to meet him. Erna came sneaking behind, even though she had been told to stay back. No way was she going to let Elizabeth face this man by herself! He saluted smartly.

"Can I help you," Elizabeth asked?

"No, but I think I can help you. I have news of your husband."

"Oh!" Elizabeth's hand flew to her mouth, she was shaking.

"He is a prisoner of war in Germany. I am sorry to have to tell you that." So saying, he turned his horse and galloped away.

Weeping, Elizabeth returned to the house.

Erna put an arm around her. "Don't cry Lisa, he will get out and come home."

"I pray so, Erna, I pray so."

On November 7, 1917, Bolsheviks, led by Lenin, seized the government. Erna was nine. Civil war would last until 1920. Russia became a communist state. The beginning of the revolution ended Russia's participation in World War I. Germany forced Russia to sign a humiliating treaty which gave much territory to the central powers. About this time the United States entered the war. Cadets, trained by Bill, were sent to fight.

Suddenly, Emil arrived home. Everyone was overjoyed. When Emil heard what had happened concerning Mount Ararat, he was not so overjoyed. From then on he nurtured an increasing hatred toward communism that he would nurture throughout his life.

Civil war spread throughout the country. Friends and relatives found themselves fighting each other. Many didn't even know what they were fighting for or against. Slowly the Bolsheviks gained the upper hand. Law became obsolete. Combatants took and did what they wanted. People were shot on the spot!

The village classroom was quiet. Then a horrible scream filled the room. All work stopped. Erna and the other students looked out the window and saw a man running toward the school. Behind him galloped several Bolshevik soldiers. They were laughing and shouting, guns drawn, arms waving.

"What's happening!" shouted the students.

"Please, take your seats and remain quiet," demanded the teacher. "Do exactly as I tell you and it will be okay."

A shot rang out. A bullet crashed through a window sending glass flying in every direction.

Some students screamed. Others ducked under the desks and benches.

"All of you, down, under your desks, and be quiet! Everyone quiet!" Shouted the teacher.

Shaking, some of them crying, they did as told. Erna put her arm around a sobbing girl. "Don't cry. It will be okay." Together they crouched under one desk, hanging onto each other.

Then the door burst open and the man ran in. His eyes were wild and his face deathly pale. He gasped for breath. Behind him came two soldiers, yelling obscenities and pointing their guns at the man. Cornered, the man's eyes swept the room. He hadn't realized until then that he had entered a school. Seeing the sobbing children he quickly put his hands in the air, faced his pursuers, and surrendered.

The teacher resolutely straightened her shoulders and said, "You can leave him here. We'll take care of him."

The man flashed her a grateful look. The soldiers laughed.

"We'll leave him here all right, madam. We'll leave him as a number one lesson to your class to never cross us! We rule!"

So saying they grabbed the man and shoved him to the front of the room, ignoring the teacher's pleas.

"To your seats, all of you!" shouted the leader to the teacher and children.

The terrified students obeyed and sat on their benches, heads hanging, shoulders sagging, trying to be as inconspicuous as possible.

"Sit up straight!" shouted the leader.

The children obeyed. Some of them stuffed their hands in their mouths to keep from crying.

The man was standing at the front of the room, arms in the air. Two soldiers raised their rifles.

"Please, please, not in front of the children," begged the man. I'll do anything you say, take me any place else, but not in front of the children."

The soldiers paid no heed.

"This village," said the leader, needs to be taught a lesson. They need to learn to listen and obey, to conform to regulations. What better place to start than with the young ones?" He turned to face the class.

"This is a lesson for you. You do what you're told. You keep your mouths shut, and your actions directed to the law, or you see what happens to you."

The teacher wondered, "What law?" But she said nothing.

"Fire!" shouted the leader.

Two guns cracked simultaneously. Blood splattered the wall, the floor, the teacher's desk. The man slumped to the floor. His face struck the desk as he fell. Children, no longer able to contain themselves began to scream. Erna's friend, fainted. Erna couldn't move. She sat staring at the sight in horror. The sight became forever etched in her mind.

The teacher and several students became sick. Gagging and heaving, they tried desperately not to throw up. The teacher knew she had to control herself for the sake of her class. Ignoring the screams and barking orders, the head soldier marched out, followed by the others. Two of them wrapped a classroom rug around the man and took him with them. With a quivering voice she tried to calm the class. As soon as the horsemen left she took them out of the room and placed them in a group, on the ground, outside. When they regained control of themselves, they were sent home, the stronger ones helping the weaker. The teacher was left to face the bloody classroom, and wonder if she might have done something to prevent this tragedy.

Elizabeth was surprised to see Erna home from school so early.

"Home already?" Then she noticed that Erna's was sickly pale. "What's wrong. Are you sick?"

Erna threw herself into Elizabeth's arms and cried with great gasping sobs.

"Oh Lisa! oh Lisa!"

"What is it? What's wrong Erna?"

"They shot a man. They shot him, Lisa. He's dead."

"Who shot who, Erna? What are you talking about?"

"The soldiers, in the school, shot a man."

Elizabeth listened to the horrible story. She could not believe that anyone could be so cruel as to deliberately subject a group of children to such a criminal act. Her heart cried within Erna as she held her tight. How she wished Otto were here to help her now. To feel his protecting arms around her. She wondered what terrible things he was going through as a prisoner of war in Germany.

Emil could no longer endure the acts of the Bolsheviks. He decided to fight them from the inside. To that end he worked undercover in an office where he pretended to be a Communist. Their he sabotaged whatever Communist intentions he could by altering orders and other paper work that would advance their cause. With his education, and political skills, he found this easy to do, though dangerous. His efforts saved many lives.

Erna's next experience with Bolshevik soldiers occurred during a raid on the home farm. Erna, Elizabeth and her son were in the orchard, picking fruit when Erna heard the sound of the galloping horses. She froze and then began to scream in terror as she spotted them coming down the lane into the farm yard. Elizabeth ran to her.

"It's okay Erna - Shhhh. Let's sit down and be real quiet."

They crouched behind a bush. Elizabeth felt guilty. She was leaving Alwina and John's wife to deal with the situation alone.

They waited for what seemed forever before the soldiers finally came out of the house. They were shouting and laughing. The raid was mainly for food, but in a wagon, pulled by horses, they spotted Alwina's bicycle.

Erna jumped, pointing, "look!"

"Quiet! I see. Be real still."

Bikes were an expensive and scarce commodity in Russia. Alwina was an excellent seamstress. She used her bike to travel around the village on errands, and making extra money with her sewing.

As soon as the soldiers were out of sight, all three jumped from their hiding place and ran for the house. Alwina was sitting at the table, her head down on her arms, sobbing.

Elizabeth ran to her. "Did they hurt you? Are you okay?"

"They never touched me. I'm okay, but they took my bike, my beautiful bike."

Everyone felt sorry for Alwina. They knew how she treasured her bike.

The fighting became worse. The village tried to protect themselves. They began hiding food and erecting barricades on roads they knew the Bolsheviks had to use. Windows and doors were barricaded. Families joined together and took up arms. Cannons were used by both sides and children could no longer go to school or play outside. Bullets and cannon shot could fly through any one's yard at any time. John joined the army against the Communists. Henry was left to look after the home place. Not much could be done on the farm anyway. Elizabeth and her children stayed at the home place, going to their place only to do necessary chores. Henry would then accompany them.

One day they were all surprised to see John running up the drive way toward the house. Everyone ran to meet him.

"John, John, your home! How wonderful!"

"Can't stay. The Bolsheviks have broken our lines. They're making raids for horses. Must get my horse out of here and hide him. You get inside and don't show your faces, any of you."

John had a beautiful and valuable stallion. They knew this was the horse he would try to hide.

"John be careful," Elizabeth screamed as they charged back for the house.

"Don't get shot, John. Don't get shot," cried Erna as she ran toward the house.

Within five minutes John and his horse were galloping out the driveway. The family braced themselves for the arrival of the soldiers. They waited and waited. No soldiers.

"I wonder what happened to them?" They looked at each other, fear on their faces.

As it was beginning to turn dark, and still no soldiers, they began to wonder if they could light a lamp. As they were debating the issue, Erna screamed, "It's John, John's coming, I see him."

John, walked up the lane, without the horse.

Elizabeth squinted. "He's sure walking funny."

They all ran to meet him. As they got closer they were stunned. His clothes were all ripped and he was covered in blood. Henry grabbed him to keep him from falling.

"They caught me. Took my horse and bull whipped me."

All his wife could say was, "But at least your alive, at least your alive. I thought you might be dead."

John reached out a shaking hand toward her. Tears welled up in his eyes.

Chapter 4

Revolution

In 1918 World War I drew to a close. But the Russian Revolution continued for two more years. Fighting became worse as family members and former friends fought each other. Many did not know why they were fighting or even who they were fighting. Many fought merely to stay alive. Neighbours and friends became suspicious of each other. No one knew who was on what side or who might betray whom in order to save his own life or the life of a family member.

Yet in the middle of great turmoil, God brings events that give us peace and the will to continue to live. Such events lighten our load and help us to know that life is sacred and to be respected, revered, and valued. So it was that a wedding, again took place in the family. Henry married the sister of the girl who had been Bill's girlfriend before he left for the United States. Every one was overjoyed and welcomed her into the family.

Henry, like Emil, could play the guitar and was an excellent singer. The village continued to hold their church services with Henry leading the choir. Whenever and wherever he could get a group together, he would lead them in song. This helped people forget their troubles and, for awhile anyway, feel like life was as it used to be. The whole family loved music and would eagerly join Henry.

When fighting drew close to the village, the people would gather in basement shelters. Since the family had a large house with a large basement, many people sought protection with them. One day canon fire came near the village. The constant noise was grueling, causing strain, exhaustion, and fear. About twenty people gathered in the family basement to wait out the shooting so they could return home. Henry had a sing song going in an attempt to drown out the noise of the battle and lessen the fear.

Suddenly a canon ball burst through a boarded-up window. Splinters flew in every direction. People ducked for cover as piercing cries of surprise and terror echoed throughout the basement. Then came a screech of agony and pain.

As Erna turned toward the sound, blood sprayed over her, and lying a few feet away was an unattached arm. Erna screamed. Then she saw the girl beside her was missing her arm.

"Oh no! Oh no! Lisa, Lisa!" screamed Erna.

Elizabeth grabbed some towels and ran for the girl. With the help of others they put pressure on the arteries to halt the bleeding. Sterilized string was used to tie off the wound. It was then bandaged in clean rags and left to heal. This was the only 'doctoring' the girl received. She would live on minus an arm.

Alwina took Erna to another part of the basement to clean the blood off of her.

"Alwina, what will happen to her?" Erna sobbed.

"She'll be all right. Lisa will look after her."

"But what if she dies?"

"She won't die. Lisa is smart. She will see that she doesn't die." Alwina silently prayed that it would be so.

Erna would never forget that terrible scene. It would from then on haunt her memories.

As the revolution continued people died so fast that coffins could not be made fast enough to fill the demand. Family, neighbours, and friends began buying linen bags to put the bodies in for burial. Alwina was often called upon to sew up these bags. She was getting orders from people she didn't even know, from great distances. It was hard to purchase the linen for the bags. Without her bike it was slower shopping as well. Since Elizabeth and the children were at the farm nearly all the time, Elizabeth helped with the work while Alwina sewed. Erna sat and helped Alwina by holding the material.

One day there came a knock at the door. Someone had arrived at the door without being seen or heard. The children became dead silent. The women stared at each other with fear in their eyes. Alwina went to the door. A shaking, tearful man stood there.

"Please madam, I need to buy five body bags, my wife, my children...." he choked up and could say no more.

Elizabeth, who had now come to the door, put her arm around him. "Come in. Have a coffee. We'll discuss it."

Gratefully the man sank into a chair and greedily gulped down the coffee and cake set in front of him. The women looked at each other.

"Would you like some bacon and eggs?"

The man's face lit up. "Well I guess I haven't had anything to eat for a couple of days. I would appreciate that."

"How did you get here?"

"Walked. No way else. Soldiers took everything."

"How did your family die?"

"Not sure. Just all got sick and died."

The women again looked at each other. In their minds they could see and smell the bodies awaiting the return of this man to bury them. They were horrified.

"Was there no relatives or neighbours to help you?"

"No. All scared of the disease."

Alwina instinctively backed away from him.

"This is all the money I can offer you," continued the man, holding out his hand.

Alwina saw that the money would hardly cover the cost of the linen if she could even get any.

"I don't know what to say to you. I have no linen and can't get any more right now."

He hung his head. "Perhaps some other kind of material?"

"I will see what I can do," said Alwina sadly.

Alwina found the strongest material she could and sewed five bags for him. He stayed that night and gratefully set out early the next morning.

Later, Henry reported that a strange flu virus was going around and that people were beginning to die from it. It seemed that all the deaths and hardships were causing much sickness. The sickness was intensified by lack of medicine.

The flu did indeed reach epidemic proportions. John, being the one most in contact with other people, was among the first to get it. He became violently ill, throwing up and gagging even when he hadn't eaten a thing. Tea and herbs were administered with no result. He continued to run a high fever. Faithfully his wife nursed him, doing her best to keep the fever down. The children were kept strictly away from the sick area.

John was a very strong man. Slowly, he began to recover. But then his wife took sick. John returned to the army, leaving Elizabeth to care for her. She got weaker and weaker. Elizabeth, try as she might, could not get her to keep anything down and her fever was out of control.

One morning at breakfast Elizabeth asked Henry if he would try to locate John and bring him home.

"Why?" asked Henry.

Tears welled up in Elizabeth's eyes. "Because I don't think she's going to make it. She needs him."

Erna was the only one of the children who understood what Elizabeth meant. She sat staring into space, shivering and filled with fear.

Henry left immediately and, with little trouble, was able to locate John. He brought him back as quickly as possible, but they were too late. John's wife died moments before they arrived home.

Alwina sewed up a body bag, and with great sorrow John's wife was buried in the village cemetery. Those at the funeral were shocked at the amount of new graves. They could not have imagined it without actually being there. Many graves had no markers.

Elizabeth, unwell herself, attended the funeral. The next morning she started suffering severe symptoms of the flu. Erna heard her vomiting in the bathroom. In terror she ran to Alwina and told her to come quick. "Lisa is sick."

Alwina ordered Erna to be quiet and get back to bed. She would help Lisa. Erna returned to bed but could not sleep. Her pillow became wet with tears. What if Elizabeth dies too? What would she do? She would want to die too.

Alwina was now in charge. Not only did she have to nurse Elizabeth and take care of the children, but she had to also run the household and do chores. She no longer had time to sew. John stayed home and Henry looked after Elizabeth and Otto's place. Alwina was so thankful for Henry's new wife.

Elizabeth did not improve. She couldn't eat. Nothing stayed down, not even water. Her fever began to soar and she became very weak. Then Alwina caught Erna in the bedroom.

"You get out of here at once!" Alwina demanded, "and don't let me catch you in here again!"

"But... But...."

"You heard me! Scoot! Now!"

"But I only wanted to help Lisa."

"Well you can't help her. Now move it!" Alwina screamed at her.

With tears coming fast, Erna fled.

Alwina's conscience got the better of her. Why had she snapped like that? Things must be really getting too much. She found Erna lying on her bed sobbing. Alwina sat down on the side of the bed and put her hand across Erna's back.

"I'm so sorry, Erna. Please don't cry. I know you just want to help Lisa, but I don't want you getting sick too."

The sobbing subsided and suddenly both sisters were in each others arms. Erna reluctantly agreed to stay out of Lisa's room.

Elizabeth's condition rapidly deteriorated. She seemed to know that she wasn't going to make it.

"Alwina, can you sit beside my bed for a minute," said Elizabeth

Alwina pulled up a chair. Elizabeth reached out and clasped Alwina's hands tightly.

"Alwina, when Otto comes home please tell him I love him very much."

Alwina made a move to protest that Elizabeth would get better.

"No, no Alwina, listen to me. I know. Please tell him."

Alwina nodded.

"And promise me Alwina, promise me that you will take care of my baby and Erna."

"I promise. "Alwina whispered.

She closed her eyes and a peaceful expression came across her face. That night God took her home to be with Him. Erna had lost her second mother. She was eleven years old.

In spite of all the hardships, sorrow, sickness, and troubles many people came to the funeral. Elizabeth was known and loved throughout the village, and numerous other villages as well. They came to give their last respects. Erna clung to Alwina. She no longer cried. She had shed too many tears before to be able to cry anymore. All she felt was a numbness inside, a huge frozen blank hole that seemed to possess the very being of her soul. Only God could know the extent of her loss, pain, and distress.

The flu epidemic spent itself and the rest of the family were spared.

The civil war in all its ferocity and cruelty continued undaunted by the epidemic. Inhumanity reigned. The cannons continued to fire day and night, blasting vengeance on guilty and innocent alike. Did they never sleep? Did they never rest?

The continuing fear and noise hammered on minds until thinking became unrealistic, unclear, a nightmare with no beginning and no end. Such was the case of the village when fighting was at it's highest peak. The village was surrounded by Bolsheviks. The defenders battled back, doing their best to protect themselves and the village. The cannons had been blasting all night long. As morning dawned, the communists broke through and thundered through the village.

People were ordered out of their homes into the yards and roadways. Houses were ransacked and plundered. Some things the victors took, other things were destroyed. Women were ravaged, some no more than children. Screams of terror and pain echoed throughout the village.

A group of about thirty people hid in the basement of the home place. Quietly, with hands held high, they filed out into the yard. One man went out of his mind. Screaming in terror he threw himself, writhing, onto the ground. He was an elderly man, his hair white with age. Alwina kept Erna behind her, protecting her from the eyes of the offenders. Those eyes were now turned upon the man on the ground.

"He's no good. Why are you keeping him here? Shoot him!"

So saying, a shot rang out. The man lay still. Laughing and yelling they left. No one else was harmed. Perhaps this man, by losing his life, saved others. Perhaps because everyone else stood quietly, they were spared. For what ever the reason they escaped persecution, they had more to be thankful for than others in the village.

As the year 1920 rolled in, the Revolution came to an end and Russia became a totalitarian communist State with the Bolsheviks in complete control. Some celebrated, others slumped into depression.

In 1922 Lenin suffered a severe stroke. In 1924 he died, causing the tide of communism to change directions. Control over the people become even more severe with Stalin at the helm.

Just before Lenin's death, prisoners of war were released from Germany. Otto returned home. Erna threw herself into his arms.

"Oh Otto, your home at last! Lisa died, Otto."

Otto turned deathly white. "What are you saying?"

Alwina took Otto's arm and escorted him to a chair. He was thin and sickly. She could feel his bones sticking out.

"I am so sorry Otto. It's true. Lisa died in the flu epidemic only a short while ago."

Otto put his head down in his hands and began to sob.

Erna and Alwina put their arms around him, trying to offer comfort.

Alwina could not believe this was the same man who marched off only a few short years ago.

"Her last words were to tell you she loved you," said Alwina.

"Thank you, Thank you so much."

"Your not well Otto," said Alwina.

"No, not well. I got a bone disease while fighting in the swamps."

"You must have had a terrible time."

"Yeah. Still can't believe it all. Doctors in Germany gave me some treatments before releasing me. Can't say I think that it helped any though."

Alwina cooked up a big meal for him. That night the whole family sat up until early in the morning talking about all that had happened. Otto insisted he was going back to his own place, even though everyone thought that he shouldn't, at least not for awhile. He said he needed to in order to sort out his life and begin again.

A couple of days later he left the home place and returned to his own farm. Alwina would spend a lot of her time there, cooking for him and trying to get his health back to normal. Erna and Otto's boy always went along. It wasn't long before everyone began thinking of them as a separate family unit. Otto's thoughts, too, began to turn in that direction. One evening, after the kids went to bed, he went to the home place to see Alwina.

"Well hi! What are you doing here so late?" asked Alwina.

"Just wanted to talk to you," Otto replied.

"Great. Always enjoy your company."

Otto blushed. "Do you think we could go for a walk?"

"Sure." Alwina wondered why he looked so strange. He wasn't usually so reserved toward her.

They strolled along chatting. Then suddenly Otto stopped, put his hands on her shoulders and said, very quickly, "Alwina will you marry me?"

"What?"

"Will you marry me?"

Alwina blushed. She was speechless.

"Well? Come on, answer my question."

"But Otto, you don't love me."

Otto put his arms around her, drawing her close to him. "Yes I do, Alwina. I do, very much."

"But your love was for Lisa."

"Yes, I loved Lisa, but she's gone, Alwina, and your here, and now I love you. That doesn't mean I don't still love Lisa. I do. But your a different person, Alwina, and I love you for yourself. Please say yes."

Alwina felt herself being drawn tight against him. Slowly she relaxed as she whispered, "Yes Otto, yes."

Once again happiness entered the household. Alwina and Otto were married. The whole village celebrated. Erna went to live with Alwina and Otto, where she had once lived with Lisa and Otto. She was happy. She now had a 'third mother.' She had developed into a very responsible girl who was not afraid of hard work and the challenges of life. This was to stand her in good stead for the years and future demands she was to encounter.

These demands were to begin almost immediately. Shortly after the marriage, Otto's bone disease returned with a vengeance.

"What's wrong, Otto?" Erna asked. She was the first to notice that Otto was limping badly and didn't look well.

"Oh, nothing much. Legs seem to be aching a bit."

"Let's take a look at them," demanded Alwina.

"Oh, don't fuss. I'll be okay."

"No really, let's see," Alwina insisted.

Sighing, Otto sat down and pulled up his pant legs. One leg was cold and blue. All three stared in disbelief.

"Its your blood circulation. We must find a doctor," said Alwina.

"And just how do you expect to do that?"

"I don't know, but I'll sure try."

Alwina did get in touch with a doctor who arrived two weeks later, looking tired and over-worked. But it was too late. Otto was sent to a city hospital where his leg was amputated.

Two years later he lost his other leg. Erna remembers last seeing him walking around on two wooden legs with crutches. Soon after she left Russia. She later got a letter from Alwina telling her that the disease had gone to his left arm. He refused to have it amputated and he died of gangrene shortly afterward. The war had claimed another victim.

The iron fist of Communism, under Stalin, began to tighten its grip. As successor to Lenin, Stalin changed everything and everyone to glorify the state and the state only. The name 'Stalin' means 'man of steel' and was the name he gave himself. All farms were to become state owned. To this end the army would be put to use. The secret police were formed to 'purge' the country of anyone opposing Stalin's ideas. The Russian Orthodox Church, through a new formed policy, was made an instrument of the state. All other churches were forbidden. Schools could only teach Communism. Instruction was rigid. Dictatorship was complete!

John called the family together. Everyone knew that they could not survive as they had been, that changes had to be made, and made right away. Everyone was frightened. The decisions made now would govern the courses of their lives in the future. It was with solemn faces that they assembled at the home farm. Conspicuously absent was Emil. "Why wasn't he here," Erna mused, "he certainly should be." She felt slightly angry that he wasn't.

"I suppose everyone has heard what happened to Emil?" said John.

"I didn't," said Erna. "What happened?"

Erna was now seventeen. She was a beautiful petite teenager, not five feet tall. Being that short would always be an annoyance for her. Her hair was long enough that she could sit on it, its color was fair.

"Emil was arrested by the secret police last night."

"Oh no!" Erna said, turning pale.

"Yeah. Seems someone informed the communists that he really wasn't one—that he was actually working against them."

"Who told you?" asked Alwina.

"A friend who works in the same office as Emil. He told me. He came to see me at about three this morning."

They all sat quietly for a moment, staring at each other. What would happen to Emil? Would there be recompenses against the rest of them for it?

"What did they say they were arresting him for?" asked Henry?

"I'm not sure that they know his complete involvement against them. Seems he was just arrested for helping people leave the country. The guy said that he probably would be sent to one of Stalin's new collective farms in Siberia where he would be sentenced to hard labour.

Henry winced. "That could be worse than prison."

"Let's hope not," said Alwina.

"Now, speaking of farms, you all realize that the government is going to take over all of our farms. We will have nothing left. All that we can do is keep our mouths shut and work for the communists, if we want to survive. Except …."

"Except what?"

"We could leave Russia."

"Where would we go?"

"How about Canada?" said John. "I've got some good information about the freedom in that country. Seems you can have free land as well. One just has to establish a farm on it and work it. Sound good?"

"Must be some catch," said Jacob, the oldest son. "Think my family and I will take our chances here."

"Well, we can't go. Otto is too ill for such a venture," said Alwina.

Henry spoke next. "Think I'll stay awhile," said Henry. "You going for sure?"

"Yes." John reached for his wife Freda's hand. Since his first wife died of the flu he had remarried. She was expecting a baby and it would be hard for her. "We have decided. We will have nothing here, so we may as well have nothing there. At least we'll have the freedom to build ourselves up again."

"I'll help you get away. You can let me know how things go and I'll follow later," said Henry.

"Thanks Henry. How about you Erna? Want to come with us? We sure could use some help with the kids." John had three children from his first wife and his second wife was expecting her third.

Erna looked at Alwina.

"You go if you want to Erna. It would be an excellent opportunity for you. There's nothing here for you," encouraged Alwina.

"But I don't want to leave you alone."

"Don't worry about me. I'll manage just fine"

Erna sat, head hanging, not knowing what to do or say. Finally, she raised her head high and said, "Thank you John. Yes, I will go with you." She had been helping to look after John's children for some time and did not want to see them go without her. She especially felt responsible for the three belonging to his first wife. It was like they were her own children. She just could not see them go without her.

The family sat for a long time, that evening, discussing their present situation, what they were going to do, and above all, what would happen to Emil. As much as they wanted to try to help him, they knew they couldn't. It would only bring a similar fate to the rest of them. It was a hopeless feeling, knowing there was absolutely nothing they could do and no one they dared even turn to for help. No one knew who to trust anymore.

Emil was sent to Siberia, but not to the hard labour farms. At first he was sent to a prison. Later he was transferred to the hard labour projects. He saw thousands of people brought in to these projects. He would see thousands killed, or die of weakness from exhaustion and lack of food. Disease killed many too.

In spite of interrogation, torture, beatings, and little food, Emil survived. He wrote many stories, some plays, and some books about his experience while there. These would always be disguised as fiction and written by different people to whom he dictated his stories. This was to disguise his hand writing as he had a unique and beautiful style of writing that could be easily recognized. The material was kept hidden, with the hope that one day he would be free and could tell the world what happened to people in Stalin's Russia.

In later years Erna received in the mail one of his stories. It told of his escape from a Russian labor camp and what was taking place in Russia at the time. It was written in a Russian dialect that she could not read. For years she kept it hidden, fearing the communists would find her, or Emil, and harm them, even though she was then in Canada. At one point she tried to get it translated, but when the people translating it took an extraordinary long time she panicked and asked to have it returned immediately. As it turned out, the reason for the delay was that they couldn't translate it into English either. They had translated part of it into German.

At the time of this writing Erna has given Emil's story to the family. It has since been translated into English. Perhaps, true to Emil's dreams, it will be published.

As John was making plans to get his family and Erna out of Russia, the doors to leaving were starting to close. People were leaving by the hundreds. The Communist government had to do something to stop the exodus. Their first move was to reduce the number of people allowed to leave to only a few a week. Protests were quickly silenced. The paper work to leave became a nightmare. People were denied exit on grounds that didn't even make sense. Henry became involved in the process of getting papers for John. To this extent he would later be involved in helping others get out, to his own detriment.

While Otto was in the hospital, Alwina stayed at the home farm. One morning, as she and Erna were going to their farm to do chores, Their eyes took in a terrible sight.

"Stop Erna! Something is wrong!" said Alwina.

"What?"

"Everything's so quiet. Listen. I don't hear the chickens or ducks, and where are the dogs?"

Erna stopped and listened carefully.

"Your right. It is awfully quiet. What do you suppose is wrong?"

"I don't know. Let's sneak through the trees and look before we go into the yard."

"Okay."

As the two sisters peered through the clump of trees they gasped in horror. Lying around the yard were all their animals, dogs, chickens, ducks, and turkeys. They were all dead. Blood was splattered everywhere.

Both girls began to cry. For several minutes they could only hang onto each other and sob. As the tears ebbed, they decided to investigate. The dogs had been shot. The poultry had their heads chopped off and thrown around. The cattle and horses were shot and left lying. The house had been ransacked. Furniture was broken.

Who would do such a thing? Why? It didn't seem like anything had been taken.

It was a sad journey back to the home farm. More tears were shed as the story was related. John was wrathful, swearing vengeance on whoever was responsible. Alwina tried to calm him.

"No, John. Don't jeopardize your chances of leaving here. You must get out. We will manage."

John did find out that communist soldiers were responsible. It seemed that they thought, since there was no one around, that the owners had fled the country. With that assumption, they took their rage out on all that was around them, destroying it all.

John felt apprehension as he waited for papers to leave Russia. It seemed to be taking forever. What if the papers didn't come? He mustn't think that way. The idea would drive him crazy. He must keep a positive attitude. Every day they discussed what they would take with them. Their ideas ranged from piles of belongings to nothing. Frantically he and Henry worked with known officials in high places to try to receive permission to exit.

Then, another setback. A typhoid epidemic broke out in the village. Hastily the quarantine signs appeared. Would this further delay their departure? Only John and Henry ventured off the property. Everyone else was told to stay put and not go anywhere. Again disease ravaged the area. In the middle of the epidemic, John's papers arrived. The family was ecstatic. They actually were going to get to go. In spite of their happiness, a sadness remained for those who would be left behind.

With the papers came a warning. They would be allowed to take only one suitcase each, plus enough money to get them to Canada. Nothing more, nothing to get them started in a new land. At first John felt devastated, then angry. All his life he had worked hard for what he had. Now he was told, in essence, that it really wasn't his at all, that it belonged to the State. If he wanted to leave he could take nothing. Then again, if he stayed, he would have nothing. Frustration reached it's peak as he stormed around the house trying to calm himself, to reason with himself, to tell himself that people were what really mattered in this world, not things or worldly possessions.

Reconciliation with himself finally arrived and he called the family together.

"We're leaving tomorrow. I think we better go quickly while we have the chance. Each person is allowed one suitcase only. Pack tonight."

Erna was shocked. "Just one suitcase each?"

"I'm afraid that's all."

"But what about all my stuff?"

"Guess you'll have to leave it with Alwina."

There was no backing out now. They were going! The packing was done. Small treasures were hidden away between clothes. Each suitcase was stuffed.

Alwina sat well into the night sewing some secret pockets into John's clothes. He had decided to try to take some extra money. He could not see them making it on what he was told they were allowed. Emergencies were bound to come, especially with small children. He was hoping the children would distract attention from himself.

Good-byes were said that evening. Early the next morning they left their ancestral home to board a train that would take them to Moscow. It was 1926 and Erna was seventeen years old.

Chapter 5

Escape

The train was old. It offered no luxuries or comforts. It rattled and banged along at a snail's pace. The seats were plain uncomfortable benches, but the children didn't seem to mind. Everyone was too excited to even think of complaining. No food was served on this train. John and his family brought their own food along with a few blankets and quilts mostly for the children. Their suitcases were jammed in along side of them. John was keenly aware of the extra money sewed into his clothes. What if it should be discovered? Erna was too thrilled to be thinking that anything might go wrong. She busily looked after the children and enjoyed the trip. But the nights were difficult. Trying to sleep on the train was no fun!

It was most difficult for John's expectant wife. The shaking of the train seemed to get worse the further they went. Then she got sick to her stomach. Erna was the first to notice something wrong.

"Are you all right, Freda?" asked Erna, "You look really pale."

"Just feeling a little under the weather," said Freda, "kind of sick to my stomach."

"That don't sound good," said John. "The baby isn't due yet for a couple of months."

Freda tried to laugh. "Don't worry. This baby is waiting for Canada. It wants freedom!"

Her words were no sooner out when she had to run for the washroom. Erna followed her. The sickness didn't pass. By the time the train reached Moscow, everyone knew that the baby was not going to wait for Canada.

In Moscow, a kindly old gentleman offered to help get Freda to a hospital. He first took Erna and the children home to his wife. Little did he realize just how much he was getting himself in for! It was well into the night before John and the gentleman arrived home from the hospital. Erna, who had not been able to sleep, met them as they entered the apartment.

"Is Freda okay?" Erna asked John.

"Yes. She's going to be all right."

Erna breathed a sigh of relief. "And the baby?"

"The baby is doing great."

"Is the baby here then? Did the baby come?"

John beamed. "Yep. We have a baby girl for you to look after."

"That's wonderful, John!" said Erna, throwing her arms around his neck, "Oh, I am so happy."

By this time the rest of the household was awake. The children happily jumped about. It was sometime before Erna got them all back to sleep.

This wonderful elderly couple asked the family to stay with them until Freda and the baby could travel. John gratefully accepted the invitation. He had not realized how difficult it would be travelling with five children. Now there would be six.

The baby was named Mary.

Just when everything seemed to be going fine, John's second oldest boy began experiencing severe headaches. He had headaches before, but now, they became extremely painful. He cried so much that Erna exhausted herself trying to comfort him.

The gentleman with whom the family was staying expressed deep concern for the boy.

"You know John," he said, "Now that you're in Moscow, close to good doctors, you should have them take a look at that boy. Might save you some trouble later on."

"Well—I don't know. Everyone has headaches sometime in their life." John was thinking of the expenses they were already incurring.

"Within normal, but this boy's don't seem normal to me. He also seems to have an extraordinary large head for such a small child."

John stared at the boy. Why hadn't he noticed before? His head did seem out of proportion to the rest of his body.

Erna also eyed the child. She had noticed the size of his head before but thought nothing of it. Now she could see that it really didn't seem normal.

Erna said, "Maybe you should get him checked. The doctor might be able to give us something to relieve the headaches until he outgrows them."

"Your probably right," said John sighing in frustration. "We'll stop tomorrow on our way to the hospital."

The prognosis was not good. More than one doctor inspected the x-rays and could not believe what they saw! The child was five years old and had a brain the size of a grown man's. They would have to operate immediately. Without an operation the child would die. Even with an operation his chances were slim.

John turned to Erna. "How am I ever going to tell Freda?"

"You have to, John. You have to discuss it with her first. The decision has to be made by both of you. He's her child too."

"I know, Erna. Your right again. But it's so hard when she's still in the hospital herself."

Both decided on the operation to give the child a chance however slim. Erna and John stayed at the hospital with Freda during the operation. The elderly couple looked after the rest of the children.

The child died on the operating table. Freda cried herself sick. Neither John nor Erna could comfort her. She was unable to go to the funeral. The child was buried in a small, obscure cemetery attached to a little church in Moscow. The elderly couple used to attend the church before the Communists came to power and outlawed church attendance.

As Erna stood beside the grave she thought of all their family, relatives and friends, who should be here but couldn't. A message had been sent home telling what had happened, but they all knew no one would even receive it on time. She thought about Elsa, her older sister. Elsa had just married before they left. As part of their honeymoon, the newly weds had come to the train station to see them off. She hadn't seen Elsa for a long time. It was a wonderful surprise. They had been so happy. What was happening now? Why were things changing so suddenly?

John decided they needed something to take their minds off of their tragedy, while waiting for Freda and baby Mary to get out of the hospital. He concluded that a tour of Moscow would be appropriate. They would probably never have another chance to see Moscow. Their host accompanied Erna and John while the children remained at home.

Erna was fascinated with the city, but what would forever remain in her mind was viewing Lenin in his coffin in his mausoleum in Red Square. Admission was charged for this 'special privilege.' Lenin lay in a glass coffin, his body completely preserved. Soldiers guarded the body day and night.

Erna stared and exclaimed, "That's perfectly horrible, John!"

"Shhhh!" John looked around, hoping no one heard. They had enough trouble already. It appeared that no one had, even so, he was sweating, as was their host.

It suddenly dawned on Erna how close she had come to getting them into difficulty. She would have to watch every word she said from now on as long as they remained in Russia.

"Sorry, John. I understand."

"That's okay, you'll learn."

"I hope not the hard way."

John gave a nervous laugh. "I hope not too." As quickly as they dared, they left. Erna shivered, glad to be away from there.

Freda and Mary were released from the hospital. John and Erna went to pick them up. Much to every one's surprise, they were met by three Russian doctors.

"We need to talk to you before you take your baby out."

Fear filled John's mind. What now? "What's the problem doctors?"

"We have detected an abnormality in your baby's throat. She will need an operation. It would be best if it were done now before she leaves the hospital."

They could not believe their ears. Another child needing an operation. It was just too much to bear. They sat looking at each other. Tears flooded Freda's eyes.

"Is it life threatening?" asked John.

"No, but as she grows older, she will have more difficulty eating and will experience trouble with her speech. Her eating problems have already begun. It's hard to tell how fast the problem will progress."

John looked at his wife and his sister. How could they possibly postpone their trip any longer? They might not be able to leave should they delay further. Maybe they weren't supposed to leave at all?

Erna said, "I think she should have the operation."

Freda agreed. John sighed in relief. At least he didn't have to make the decision alone. Whatever was to happen would happen. So baby Mary was left at the hospital. The operation was scheduled for the following week.

Their host did not seem upset over this new turn of events. They took it all as a part of life and tried their best to comfort their adopted family.

"You know, John, there's one large church left in Moscow still holding services. Would you and your family care to attend tomorrow? Could be a comfort to you."

"Oh yes, that would be wonderful, let's go John," said Erna enthusiastically.

John smiled. "Sure, we'll go, as long as you think it's safe."

"Well, so far the church hasn't been bothered. Maybe the congregation is too large for the communists to tackle yet."

"Okay, tomorrow we'll go."

The next morning, with so many kids to get ready, they were late leaving for church. The kids laughed and skipped on their way to church. Suddenly they all stopped dead in their tracks. A group of Russian soldiers on horseback thundered down the street toward the church.

A crowd of people were walking up the wide steps leading to the entrance of the white church when the soldiers arrived, shouting obscenities and wielding whips that landed on the backs of men, women and children. Terrified, the victims screamed and ran in every direction. Some fell and rolled down the steps. Others were trampled by horses. A couple of the riders rode their horses right up the steps and into the church. Men, women, and children poured out of the church and fled through a gauntlet of soldiers who reigned further blows upon the hapless victims.

John, Erna, and Freda grabbed the children by the hands and, with their hosts, beat a hasty retreat.

"Don't run!" ordered John. "Walk like nothing happened. If we run they will know that we were on our way to church."

"Will they follow us?" asked one of the frightened children.

"I hope not," answered John. "Walk quickly, just a little further and we're around the corner and out of sight."

As they turned the corner Erna breathed a sigh of relief, but she could not restrain her tears. "Those poor people. How could God allow such cruelty?" her mind queried.

But then she remembered hearing on many occasions that "God strengthens through adversity," and she was being strengthened. In her heart came the resolution that no one, communist or otherwise, would stop her from worshipping her God. She could be just as stubborn as they. Her faith would not be shattered or broken by anyone. She only wished there was something she could do to help those other people. But she knew, for the sake of the children, they had to get away from there as fast as possible.

Baby Mary's operation was successful. Everyone rejoiced. For a couple of days John relaxed. Maybe they would get out yet. But Mary was kept in the hospital far longer than he had anticipated. As he followed the political scene closely, he worried more and more about getting out of Russia. He was sure the government would soon close the borders completely.

Finally Mary was released from hospital and John announced that they would leave the very next day for Regal, Latvia.

"Don't you think the baby should be allowed time to gather strength before you go?" asked the host.

"I would think you'd be tired of us by now," replied John with a grateful smile.

"We have enjoyed having you."

"Thank you, but I do want to leave tomorrow anyway. I'm afraid that if we linger any longer, we'll not get out at all."

"I can see that," said the host sadly.

The next morning, John gave his host a generous gift of money as a token of his gratitude. He was thankful for the extra money he had sewn into his clothes. He was also able to pay his hospital bills, but he would have very little left to cross the border. His mind was somewhat eased, however, for now there would be nothing illegal for any official to find on his person.

They had been in Moscow for three months.

Along with the excitement went apprehension, as they again boarded the train. The older children picked up the tension from John and Freda. Would they get across the border? Erna was fairly bouncing around, trying not to let the children know how scared she was. After what she had witnessed at the church, she desperately wanted to get out of Russia. Suddenly all that she had left behind didn't matter. All that mattered was getting out to freedom.

As the train pulled into the border crossing, everyone became very quiet. Soldiers entered the coach and marched up the aisles, checking papers and asking questions. One soldier took John's papers and shuffled aimlessly through them. Suddenly he stared at John.

"These papers were dated three months ago. How come your just leaving now?"

"We lost a child in Moscow. If you look closely, you will see permission for one more on there."

Again the man looked at the papers, then back at John. "I see the same number of children on the papers as I see here."

John realized his mistake. "We also had the baby born in Moscow, sir, during the three months. You can see the difference in the ages on the papers."

"Then you don't have permission for the baby to leave."

John turned pale. Erna felt sick to her stomach. Quickly she raised her hand.

Index Map of German Settlement Areas in USSR

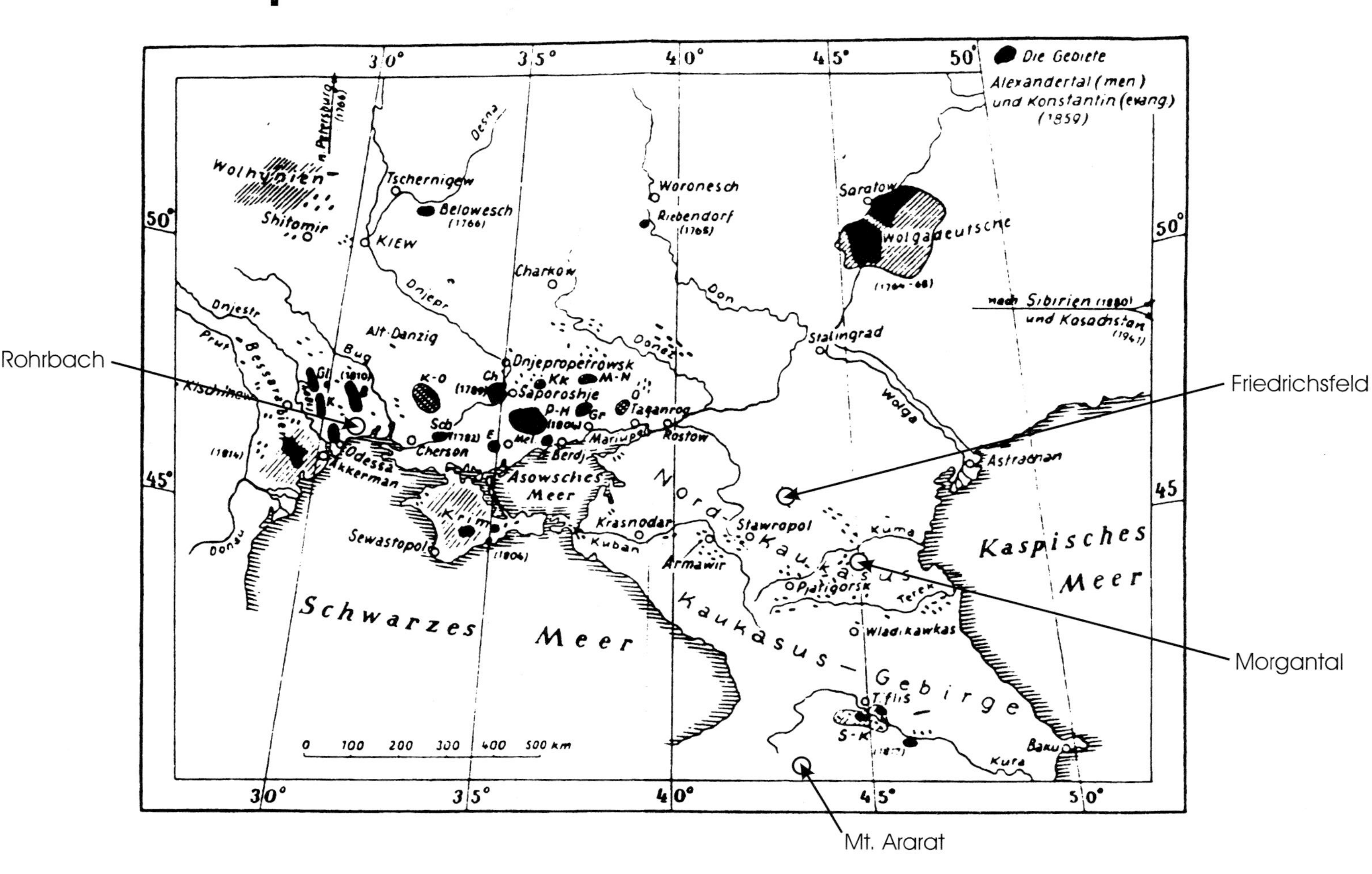

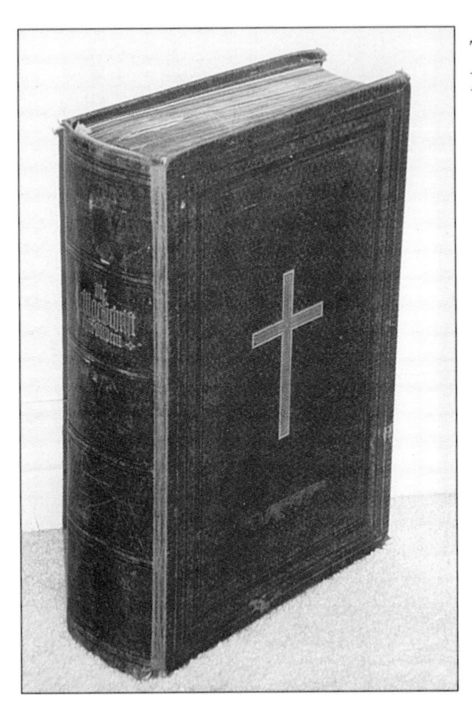

The bible given to Erna by Mrs. Hader in England.

Erna playing her seven string guitar, soon after arriving in Canada.

Erna riding horseback at her brother John's farm in Canada.

John with his second wife Freda,
and baby Mary in Canada.

Erna and Emil in their wedding clothes.
Taken beside their farm house.

Brother Emil when he
got married in Finland.

A family picture.

Erna and Emil with baby Ruby.

Daughters Ruby, Linda and Carol with pets on top of the farm house.

Part of the threashing crew. The team of horses belong to Erna and Emil.

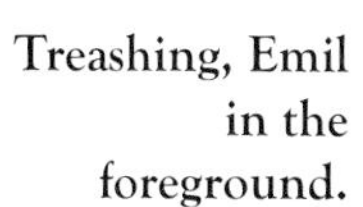

Treashing, Emil in the foreground.

Grandchildren getting a "stone-boat" ride from Emil on the farm land.

Mother's pride and joy, her children Carol, Linda, and Ruby.

Erna with daughters Ruby, Carol, and Linda.

Erna working on her handicrafts.

Erna celebrating her birthday.

Erna and Emil. Taken in June, 1978. Age 70, six years after retirement.

Where Emil was kept prisoner before his escape.

"Please sir," said Erna.

"Yes?"

"We would not want to put you through all the problems of taking care of a small baby sir, they need a lot of care, sir. I promise you, I will give the baby the best of care for you, sir, if you will be so kind as to allow the baby to go with us, sir."

The soldier looked at the beautiful teenager and smiled, in spite of himself.

"Permission granted young lady. I expect your quality of care will be the very best."

"Oh yes, thank you so much sir, thank you so much."

The soldier moved on, with heart felt thanks ringing in his ears as everyone echoed Erna's gratitude. The color was returning to John's face. He looked at Erna.

"Thanks kid. You really did it for us."

Many people were taken off the train before it finally was allowed to leave. As it moved across the border into Latvia, voices raised spontaneously in cheers from one end of the train to the other. Latvia was still an independent country. It would later lose its independence and become a Republic of the U.S.S.R. Two weeks later the border closed.

Meanwhile, Henry had become more involved with getting people out of Russia—so involved that he failed to get himself out before the borders closed. He also became involved with a girl that he would eventually marry and have a family. He continued to work on the farm he grew up on, but it no longer belonged to the family. It was now a collective farm owned and controlled by the government. But Henry was not happy in not being able to own his own place. He was angry at the communist regime for what they had done to his family, to the village, and to the whole country. His resentment did not go unnoticed.

One day Henry was told that he was being mobilized to work for the government on a special project in Siberia. He was told his family would be looked after and cared for while he was gone. In reality the special project turned out to be hard labor in the Gulag. While in the labor camps, Henry let his hair and beard grow, changing his appearance completely. He then proceeded to sneak out of the camp and return to his family. They were overjoyed to see him and he spent two wonderful weeks with them before returning to camp. No one ever heard from him again. All inquiries led to a dead end!

"Regal, Latvia!" shouted the conductor.

When the immigrants got off the train, an official ordered them to follow him.

"Where are they taking us, John?" asked Erna apprehensively.

"I don't know," said John, "but Latvia is a free country. They will probably help us get to England. From there we can go to Canada."

They were assembled in a large room. A man began to speak.

"Before you can leave for England, you will have to undergo tests. Lodging will be provided for you to stay in until you are authorized to leave."

"What kind of tests?" asked John.

"Doctors from England will give physical examinations to make sure you are carrying no diseases."

"We are not diseased!" said Erna with indignation.

"I'm sure you're not, young lady, but we have to comply with England's laws in order for you to proceed to that country. All luggage will also be checked. I wish you all the best in your journey."

They then lined up to receive rooms. John, and Freda, with their little boy and baby Mary, were given one room. Erna was assigned a room with Linda, Otto, and Ewald, children from John's first wife. The rooms were small but adequate. They were told testing would begin the next day. This would give them a chance to clean up and rest after their long train trip. Meals were provided, and they were told where to assemble and at what times.

The next day was hectic. At the end of it all they were told that the children were suffering from eye infections and they would have to stay there until the condition was cleared up. John argued, but to no avail. England would not allow them in. Another delay. Even though they were out of Russia, they were still much too close for John's comfort. He desperately wanted to be on his way and start a new life in Canada. The women and children, depending on him for guidance, were not quite as anxious. In fact, over the next little while they would enjoy their stay considerably.

They stay stretched to two months before they were allowed to proceed to England. The eye treatments, lodging, and meals were provided. It was five months since they had left home and the weather was turning cold. John had to purchase warm coats for his family. Erna still remembers hers—a beautiful brown one that she greatly cherished.

John bought her another item that was very dear to her. He came to her room grinning from ear to ear and carrying a large box.

"This is for you."

"For me? What is it?"

"Open it and see."

The shape of the box caused Erna to guess what it might be, but she couldn't believe her eyes when she opened it. It was a beautiful guitar.

"Oh John, thank you, thank you so much." She threw her arms around him, nearly smothering him in her joy.

"Your doing such a wonderful job keeping the children occupied with singing, I just thought this might help."

Erna was staring at the guitar. There was something weird about it. It finally dawned on her what it was.

"John, it has seven strings."

"Well?"

"I don't know how to play a guitar with seven strings. They normally have only six."

John's examined the guitar.

"I'll be darned. I never even noticed that."

"Could it be exchanged?"

John's face fell. "I really doubt it."

While waiting in Regal, Latvia Erna met a group of young people. Among them was a young man who knew how to play a seven string guitar. He taught Erna how to play chords and to accompany children when they sang. The guitar would come to Canada. Erna had it for years. One day John's children, now grown, would borrow the guitar. It was left on the bed and some clothes got thrown on top of it. Someone, not knowing it was there, jumped on it and smashed it to pieces.

At last the family was allowed to set out for England. Erna found it hard to believe that they were actually on their way. Even now the officials seemed hesitant about letting them go. For what reason, they couldn't understand. The children's eyes seemed good to them.

In England they were subjected to a similar battery of tests. This time rooms and meals were not provided. At the end of the examinations John was informed that his three oldest children, from his first wife, had trachoma and that it would take several months to clear it up. This was just too much for John! He didn't know where to turn or what to do.

Fortunately, they had been travelling with a group of Mennonites also on their way to Canada. They had friends and relatives in England who helped other Mennonites in transit. Upon hearing of John's plight, they offered to look into the matter. John could not express his thanks enough to these wonderful people. He gratefully accepted their offer, praying that in return, he would one day be able to help someone else.

The three children were not to be allowed to leave England for Canada until their eyes were completely cured. That was final! And John could not afford to stay in England until they were better. It was John's good fortune that the Mennonites offered to keep the children until they would be able to travel to Canada.

Erna was stunned. Lose her children? "John, maybe I could stay here with them until they can come?"

John looked at her. "That would be gratefully appreciated, Erna, but I don't want you messing up your life for me."

"Oh, don't be silly. I wouldn't be, John. Arriving in Canada a few months later won't make any difference to me."

"But I don't even have any extra money to give you."

"It doesn't matter. Maybe I can get a job, or at least a part time one, while I'm waiting for the kids to get better."

"I can't refuse. I love you Erna." John gave her a loving hug, followed by Freda's thankful one.

John, Freda, and the two smaller children left for Canada.

Erna, Linda, Ewald, and Otto, remained under the care of the Mennonites. Erna did get a job, ideal to her situation—looking after two young children, a ten-year-old boy and a seven-year-old girl, for a lady by the name of Mrs. Hader. At the same time she looked after John's three children.

Mrs. Hader's husband had recently died and she wanted to go to Canada to start a new life. She wished to go ahead of the children to get a home ready before the children came. The pay wasn't much, but it included room and board for Erna and the children, plus some spending money for Erna.

Erna met several Mennonite girls who spoke both English and German. Erna became good friends with them. They helped Erna look after the children while taking Erna on tours around England. In this way Erna got to see a lot of England and had a good time in spite of all her responsibilities.

Soon Ewald's eyes recovered and the doctor said he could leave for Canada. The Mennonites wrote to John in Canada and made arrangements for Ewald and the Hader boy to board a ship for Canada. Erna worried over sending Ewald on his own, but she was assured that the boys would be carefully supervised all the way. Besides, Mrs. Hader had said to send her son.

A short time later, Otto's eyes cleared up.

The leader of the Mennonite's approached Erna and asked: "How would you like to sail for Canada with Otto? Mrs. Hader is arriving to get her belongings and her daughter."

"But what about Linda?" asked Erna.

"We know a lady who is waiting to go to Canada to meet her husband," said the Mennonite. "She has a girl around Linda's age. Linda could stay with her and go later."

Erna talked to Linda, who agreed.

Erna was excited. At last, she would be going to Canada. She could hardly believe it!

There was just one thing she wanted to do before leaving England. She approached one of the Mennonite girls and asked: "Would you help me? I would like to get my hair cut before I leave."

The girl stared at her. "Your beautiful hair? You want it cut? Why?"

"Haven't you noticed? Everyone here has their hair short."

"But maybe they don't in Canada."

"Besides, it's so hard to take care of. It will really be in the way on the ship and once I get to Canada."

"Suit yourself, but it does seem a shame. If I could grow mine to sit on it, I sure wouldn't cut it. And the light color is so gorgeous. You would have those Canadian men falling all over you."

Erna blushed. "I really don't have time for men right now. They are so much work!"

Both girls giggled. "Yes, but worth it, don't you think?"

"Well, maybe. Anyway, I really do want my hair cut."

"Sure. One of our older ladies does a nice job of cutting hair. She'll do it for you. She would probably like to keep the hair in return."

"No problem. I sure couldn't keep it, even if I wanted to."

The elation and enthusiasm was to vanish as Erna felt the first snips of the scissors. Maybe she was wrong. Maybe she should have left it? Afterward her head felt light. She hadn't realized how thick and heavy her hair really was.

"That was all mine?"

"That it was. Hard to believe eh? Here, look at yourself," said the Mennonite woman.

Gingerly Erna took the mirror. She looked much more in style and she suddenly felt better about it. It would be okay.

"Yes—thanks. I like it."

"Well, I'm sure glad you do, because you probably will never grow it this long again."

"I suppose you're right." Erna never again wore her hair long.

Just before she was to leave England, Mrs. Hader arrived. She greeted Erna with a tremendous hug.

"How good to see you. I've got everything settled in Canada and will be following after you shortly."

"What's Canada like? Is it anything like Russia?" asked Erna.

"Not really — it's — it's — oh Erna, there's such a feeling of being able to live like you want to live. The freedom and potential, the possibilities are just tremendous. You'll love it."

"Wonderful! What's the climate like there now?"

"Well, its been so long since you've left Russia that it's now starting to turn pretty cold there. You will need warm clothes. Here's some extra money for you to buy yourself a few things. And Erna, this is for you too, for the great job you've done with my children."

Erna accepted the money and gift. "Mrs. Hader, you didn't have to get me anything."

"I know, but this is a very special gift for a very special person. Open it."

Quickly Erna ripped off the paper. Inside was a beautiful German Bible.

"Oh Mrs. Hader, thank you, thank you so much! This is the best gift ever." She threw her arms around Mrs. Hader. "I will cherish it always."

And so she did.

Erna and Otto stared in awe at the ship that was to take them to Canada. Never had they seen such a huge ship.

"Look Erna," said Otto, We get to go on it!"

"It will be a wonderful trip, Otto. We will enjoy it."

Excitement was high as they made their way onto the ship and were assigned a room of their own. Grant you, it was a pretty small room, but it would be their very own for the duration of the journey. They settled in, then went to explore the ship.

By today's standards it was actually very small. The great ocean waters tossed it about like a ping pong ball. It wasn't very long before both Otto and Erna were sea sick and taking turns running to the washroom, and wondering if they really would reach Canada after all. It was a long hard journey, but Erna, ever eager for life, kept their spirits high. She spent considerable time helping others as well. Even though her English was poor, her love of people was a universal language that everyone understood.

The ship docked at Halifax. They were not stopped or detained upon arrival, but they were greeted and helped by cheerful, relaxed people. From Halifax they boarded a train for Consort Alberta.

It was December, 1927, nearly a year after Erna left her home in Russia. Who would have believed that it would take her this long to get to Canada? She could hardly believe it herself. The train was certainly no luxury item (it was similar to the ones Erna had ridden on in Russia). It rattled and banged across Canada at a crawl. They spent their time, noses glued to the windows, watching the scenery and comparing it to Russia. At Winnipeg, snow began to fall. The further they travelled, the more snow they saw on the ground. Erna pulled her brown coat tightly about her, grateful for its warmth.

When they arrived in the little town of Consort, Alberta, Erna spotted her brother coming with a sleigh and horses. The sleigh was loaded with furniture—so loaded that it looked as if it would topple any minute. She stared hard at the sleigh. She couldn't believe it. There was her brothers Bill with John. And wasn't it just like them to load the sleigh that way. Shrieking with glee, Erna ran to meet them, Otto running right along beside her.

Chapter 6

So This Is Canada

It was a crisp, cold wintry night when Erna tore into the farm house shouting "John! Freda! Get the kids! The world is coming to an end!"

"Erna," said John looking startled, "what on earth are you screeching about?"

"It's the end! Jesus is coming!"

"Calm yourself, girl. What are you trying to say?" John put an arm around her shaking shoulders.

"Look outside, John. Look! It's the end of the world!"

"Don't be silly, Erna. Come, let's take a look."

Together they walked out into the chilly darkness.

"Look there John! See?"

Erna began to pray while John viewed the lights flashing across the sky like curtains wafting in the breeze in fantastic patterns and hues of yellow, red, green, blue, and violet. A hissing sound seemed to come from the magnificent lights that danced across the sky. At first John could just stare in awe. Then he began to laugh. Gently he took Erna by the arm.

"It's not the end of the world, Erna. It's just the Northern Lights."

"The what —?"

"The Northern Lights. They occur here often."

"But what causes them?"

"I don't know, but lets get the rest of the family so they can enjoy it too."

Erna, glanced over her shoulder, not totally convinced, and followed John into the house. Rousting the kids out of bed, Erna and John bundled them up and took them outside to see the spectacular display. The children were thrilled. It was much better than firecrackers! They watched the colours flit across the sky for over an hour. The chilled air finally drove them back inside.

Later, Erna learned that the real name of the northern lights is aurora borealis and that they are caused by electrically charged particles entering the atmosphere and colliding with air molecules. The auroras coincide with periods of greatest sunspot activity and with magnetic storms. They take place between fifty-six and ninety-seven kilometres above the earth.

Erna didn't go to sleep for a long time that night. She kept thinking about what she had seen, how she had felt, and what a great and wonderful country Canada is. She decided she wanted to see and experience as much as she possibly could.

It was this decision that determined her to look for a job. Besides, John could ill afford to support her. He, with a large family, was starting all over again, and he didn't need an extra mouth to feed. He had built a log cabin in a great hurry. It was small and everyone was severely cramped for space. Also, while in England, Erna experienced the freedom and independence that comes with earning your own way. She wanted to be on her own.

Her English was still poor. This made it difficult for her to get a job. Finally a neighboring Dutch family, operating a large farming enterprise, hired her as a domestic. Their German was similar to Erna's, so communication was good. They agreed to help her improve her English. The family also employed several men. Erna turned out to be an excellent and efficient housekeeper who got along well with the lady of the house.

One day this lady rushed into the house. She was very angry. Erna had never seen her in such a state and wondered if she had done something wrong.

"What's the matter? What did I do?" inquired Erna.

"You didn't do anything wrong, Erna. It's those useless guys out there. They can't get the mules to carry the lunches out to the men in the field. I don't know what to do. Guess they'll have to carry them out themselves. Such idiots!"

"Can I help?" asked Erna.

"I don't think so, but you can try if you wish."

As they approached the men, Erna watched one guy sitting on the mule kicking and whipping it while another was beating it on the rump. The mule stubbornly stood his ground, ears back and head down, legs braced forward, and refusing to move an inch. Another mule, loaded with the lunches and attached to the first one with a rope, stood impassively. Having suffered enough abuse, the lead mule threw his back legs into the air and sent the rider sprawling to the ground. The second man rushed to help his dazed co-worker to his feet.

"Serves you right," said Erna, her head high and disgust in her voice. "What right have you to beat this poor creature?" She walked over to the mule. Talking and petting it, she turned to the lady and said: "Let me take the lunches to the men?"

"Can you ride?"

"Of course I can. I've ridden tougher looking creatures than these. These guys are beautiful!"

"Well, if you think so." The lady sounded dubious.

By this time the mule was rubbing its head against Erna in a gesture of friendliness. With one leap Erna was on its back. Taking the reins and making little clicking noises, the mule's ears went forward and he took off, pulling the second mule behind him.

The men stood with gaping mouths and watched the procession amble away. The lady of the house laughingly called out, "I'll put these two guys to work doing your job!"

Even more astounded were the field workers when Erna arrived with their lunches. Since it was late, she pushed the mules at their utmost speed, making the dust fly around them. With a flourish she came to a halt in front of her employer.

"Well, what have we here!" A smile played on his lips.

"Your lunches, sir."

"And delivered with beauty to say the least, although a bit late."

"The men couldn't get the mules to go."

"And you could?"

"Oh yes, sir. No problem."

"Well then from now on you will be in charge of these mules and you will deliver our lunches. Would you like that?

"Would I! Oh boy, I sure would. Thank you so much," said Erna enthusiastically.

From then on handling the mules and delivering the lunches became part of Erna's daily duties. Whenever the mules were involved in something, Erna was right there. They always responded to her kind and gentle coaxing. The lady of the house complained to her husband that he was taking her hired help away from her. His reply was for her to use his. This was not a very satisfactory settlement for her. The men teased Erna about it, calling her their little wild one. She didn't mind, she was happy working with the mules.

In 1929, Erna was twenty and wanted new experiences. She had worked a year on the farm. Her next job was in the kitchen of the Consort Hotel near her brother's farm. The hotel proprietors spoke German and agreed to help Erna improve her English. They had two grown boys who worked in the kitchen and a girl still in elementary school.

Her first day on the job, Erna eyed the kitchen in dismay. It was a terrible mess! Dirty dishes, pots and pans were strewn everywhere. The two boys appeared in as bad a state as their kitchen.

Seeing Erna, they demanded, "What are you staring at?"

"At you two guys," answered Erna.

The men shifted about uncomfortably.

"Well, you can stop staring and get to work!" said one of the boys.

"You sure look like you can use some help," answered Erna. "Where did you want me to start?"

One guy tossed her an apron.

"You can finish making these pies for me."

The men grinned as Erna tried to get the huge apron to fit. It wrapped around her twice, bringing a scowl to her face. Tomorrow she would bring her own.

Erna was an excellent cook. It didn't take her long to finish the pies. Without waiting further instructions, she started cleaning up the mess. Before the week was finished, the whole kitchen was clean and organized. Instead of the boys giving orders, Erna took command of the kitchen. The boys didn't seem to mind, in fact it was a great relief to them to have someone else take on the responsibilities. They had been forever getting in trouble with their parents over their work, now things began to run smoothly.

Customers noticed the difference in the cooking and began complimenting the owners. The clientele increased. Erna, as part of her pay, was given a room of her own and all she could eat, not that she ever ate that much.

A prominent, unmarried banker also occupied a room in the hotel. Late one evening, as Erna was going to her room, they met at the bottom of the stairs. With a flourish of his hand and a little bow, he said, "Ladies first."

Erna stared at him with eyes growing huge. Then in terror she hastily retreated in the opposite direction.

"Well," wondered the young man as he watched Erna flee, "I wonder what's wrong with her."

Erna barged into the room where her employer's wife was working at her desk. Startled, she said, "Erna, what's wrong?"

"That man—that man—he propositioned me!"

"What man? What are you talking about?"

"The man that stays upstairs. He wants me to go to bed with him."

"The banker? I would never have thought such a thing of him, he seems like such a nice young man."

"Yes, yes, that's him, the banker."

"What did he say Erna?"

"He signaled with his hand for me to come, then he said ladies first to go upstairs with him." The words tumbled out.

Her listener sat looking incredulously at Erna. Then she began to laugh while Erna blushed in confusion.

"It's not funny!" She said indignantly.

"No, no Erna. That's not what I'm laughing about. You misunderstood him."

"I did?"

"Yes, you did. That's the Canadian way of saying your a lady, I will let you go up the stairs first."

"Oh no! Now what am I going to do? I am so embarrassed."

"I wouldn't do anything. Just forget about it. He won't know."

"Yes he will. I just know he will."

"I'll talk to him if you wish."

"Oh no, please, don't do that. Oh, I am feeling so foolish." Erna turned and dashed out the door mumbling, "so this is Canada," to herself. It was a long time before she was able to look at the young man without feeling self-conscious.

Erna worked approximately one year at the hotel.

Whenever and wherever there was music you would find Erna singing and sometimes playing her guitar, talking to people, learning English, and learning about Canada. This attracted other people to her.

Relatives living nearby asked her if she would work for them. They had two small children and desperately needed help. They begged Erna to quit her job and come work for them, at least for a time. Erna felt sorry for them and agreed. After all, they were relatives. Erna became so attached to the little girl that she later named 'Ruby,' her first daughter, after her.

During this time, Erna met Emil, the man destined to become her husband. When asked how she first met him she replied, "Well, I didn't just bump nose to nose with him, you know. There was a group of us young people together."

The people Erna worked for were not only relatives through marriage but also close relatives of Emil. They all attended an evangelical church in the area. A group of young people had formed a small band that performed at various church functions. Emil played tuba in the band. A friend invited Erna to one of these functions.

She was fascinated with the band and the young man who played the tuba.

"Who is the young man with the huge monstrosity of a tuba?" asked Erna.

"That's Emil." replied Erna's friend.

"Emil? "I have a brother named Emil."

"What a coincidence. I'll have to introduce you to him. Does your brother play a tuba too?"

"No, he plays the guitar and he's a beautiful singer, and yes, I'd love to meet this Emil!"

"He's very shy. Doesn't talk much, and I can't say I've ever heard him sing."

"No problem. I'll wake him up. I can talk."

Both girls laughed, enjoying their little ruse.

Erna was introduced to Emil who shyly offered his hand.

"Pleased to meet you."

"Likewise. I can't believe anyone playing an instrument that big. It must be hard to play?"

Emil shrugged, "Not really."

Erna was to find that shrug a common gesture of Emil's. He was even more shy than she could have imagined. She wasn't even sure that he liked her. She finally gave up trying to get him to talk, but not until after she had tried to play his tuba. To her utter dismay she was unable to even get a sound out of it. How embarrassing! Emil stood next to her grinning. His warm grin would become a familiar and treasured sight to Erna. He always appeared to be happy with life.

Erna started seeing a lot of Emil. Wherever she went, there he was. And he always seemed happy to see her. Yet he would never ask her for a date. She was disappointed. Then one day her employer handed her a letter.

"Emil's brother said to give this to you," he said quizzically.

She took the letter and ran to her room. The letter said that she was very beautiful and that he (Emil) would like to go out with her. He said that he really admired her but was too shy to be able to ask her out face to face, and that was why he was writing to her. It was signed Emil.

Erna's heart jumped. She read the letter again. She couldn't believe he had actually written it! Quickly, she wrote a reply, thanking him and saying she was glad he had written and she understood his shyness. Of course she would go out with him any time he wished. Happy and excited, she gave the letter to her employer to mail.

A confused expression passed over Emil's face as he read the letter. He read it several times trying to understand its meaning. He hadn't written her! Then suddenly it dawned on him.

"Sam! Oscar! come here!" he shouted.

The two younger brothers came running.

"You two wouldn't happen to know anything about a letter written to Erna, would you?"

The two brothers looked at each other and broke out laughing.

"What did she say?" They grabbed for the letter, but Emil jerked it away from them.

"You guys did this, didn't you?"

"Well, we had to do something. We know you want to date her but you just don't have the nerve."

"Yeah, your a chicken shit. Squawk, squawk." Oscar put his hands under his arms pretending to be a chicken. Emil dropped the letter and lunged at him. Sam retrieved it and an all out scuffle broke out. The ruckus brought their father onto the scene.

"What's going on in here!" he demanded.

At the sound of their father's voice the boys jerked to attention. Their dad, Jacob, ran his household with an iron hand. No one dared disobey.

"Nothing."

"Nothing much."

"I wouldn't call that noise nothing. Let me see that." He grabbed the letter and read it. "You wrote this letter, Emil?"

"No. These guys wrote her and signed my name."

"Do you want to date her?"

Emil hung his head.

"Of course he does," Oscar interjected.

"In that case, Emil, you will contact her and make arrangements. And you two" he motioned to Sam and Oscar, "will come with me!" He handed the letter to Emil who was blushing twenty shades of red.

As they followed Jacob out, Oscar and Sam held up their fingers in a victory sign, looking back at Emil, grins pasted on their faces. Even the prospects of the punishment to come could not daunt their enjoyment of the situation. Little did they know how big a favor they actually were doing Emil. He would never have gotten up enough courage to ask Erna out had it not been for his brothers. Not until years later did Erna learn that Emil hadn't written the letter.

When the people Erna was working for no longer needed her help, she found a job cooking in Castor, Alberta. Erna and her friend Anna together rented an apartment. They were paid well and often went shopping in Calgary. Although Erna didn't see as much of Emil now as before, they were still seeing each other. She was thoroughly enjoying this new country and all the advantages it had to offer her.

It was through their trips to Calgary that Erna heard about a desperate need for help at the High River Hospital. Always eager for new challenges, Erna persuaded Anna that they should go to work there. Emil wasn't happy with her decision, but he said nothing more than "It will be really hard to get to see you if you're that far away."

She told him, not to worry. "I'll visit you often."

Then she left on her new adventure.

It was 1932. Erna was twenty-four years old. She and Anna became ward aides at The High River Hospital. Their duties included changing and making beds, cleaning bed tables, putting fresh ice water in glasses, attending to babies, etc. Each was provided with their own room in the hospital basement. The rooms were comfortable, but they contained a network of pipes that hung about a foot from the ceiling. They formed various patterns, criss crossing over and around each other. Erna was fascinated with them. They reminded her of the branches on the huge mulberry tree in front of her home in Russia. She couldn't resist her childhood urges. Being small and agile, she discovered that by standing on her bed and jumping she could grab hold of the pipes. She would then pull herself up on them and do various swinging exercises across the room. How she enjoyed that!

One day, while she was sitting in a corner atop the pipes, her door flew open and the matron entered.

"Erna, are you here? I need your help." The matron had been in such a hurry she had forgotten to knock.

In a small embarrassed voice Erna replied, "yes."

The matron peered around the room. "Where are you? I don't see you."

"Up here."

"Up where?"

"Above you, in the corner."

The matron's eyes moved slowly up to the corner of the room. Erna waved sheepishly. The matron gasped. She couldn't believe her eyes.

"What on earth are you doing up there? Get down at once!"

A series of simian swings brought Erna above the bed where she jumped down.

The matron watched with mouth agape. The reason for her haste had all been forgotten.

"Erna, I can't believe what I've just seen. What are you trying to do, kill yourself?"

"No, just exercising."

"Exercising? Can't you find a safer way to exercise? What if you broke those pipes?"

"They won't break. They're really strong."

Ignoring Erna's comment she continued, "And how undignified, a girl your age doing such a thing. What would people think? Don't ever let me catch you doing that again!" She stormed out of the room, her mind completely devoid of her reason for being there in the first place.

Erna muttered, "Yes ma'am."

Then anger surged through her. It was her room, why couldn't she do as she pleased in her own room? For sure she would never catch her again, because from now on she would keep her door locked! She straightened her shoulders. With a determined look on her face, she locked her door and went back to swinging on the pipes!

The next night her door handle turned and wiggled, followed by a loud determined knock. Erna unlocked the door. It was Anna.

"Oh, so now your locking me out."

"Not really, just locking others out, a safety precaution." She noticed Anna staring at the ceiling. "What are you looking at?" demanded Erna.

Anna laughed. "Just checking your pipes for leaks. Do you really get up there and swing on those things."

"What? She told you?" Erna stormed.

"She told everyone. She's having a hay day talking about you swinging from those pipes."

Erna flopped on her bed. "How could she! How dare she tell everyone!"

"Well Erna, it really is hilarious you know."

"I don't think so!"

"Let me see you do it? I couldn't begin to do that."

"No!" Erna was pouting, upset over the idea that the whole staff knew.

And so she had reason to be upset. From then on everyone teased her unmercifully, calling her their little monkey. But that didn't stop Erna from swinging on those pipes for the three years she worked at the High River Hospital.

While working around patients, Erna would sing, especially to the children. One day a doctor overheard her. He paused to listen, then approached her.

"Erna, You have a beautiful voice. Would you like to join our church choir."

"Why thank you so much, sir. What church would that be?"

"The United Church of Canada."

"An impressive title. Yes, sir, I'll come."

"Wonderful! See you there."

Erna began attending the United Church where she joined the choir.

She had been working at the hospital for about a year when she was called into the matron's office.

"Have a chair, Erna."

"Yes ma'am." The matron was smiling so it couldn't be too bad.

"Your a great worker Erna. I appreciate all you do around here."

"Thanks ma'am."

"Your work is also very meticulous and conscientiously done. Our nurses are extremely overworked, so I would like to promote you to nurse's assistant."

Erna felt very proud, but a little scared.

"I would like you to work closer with the nurses and patients" continued the matron. "Your excellent in dealing with people and I believe you will do very well. In the event that we should be short staffed, I would like you to help out in the operating room and the case room, as well as taking over some of the personal needs the nurses administer to the patients."

Erna gasped. The operating room. Could she really help out there? And the case room? That was where babies were delivered! That would be great. She already had experience in Russia and knew a lot about birthing and the care of children.

"Don't look so stunned, Erna. You'll do a wonderful job. I know."

"Thank you. I'll do my best."

Erna remained at the High River Hospital for two more years working as a nurse's assistant. She thoroughly enjoyed her time there.

While working at the hospital, she, true to her promise, did see Emil whenever she could, mostly at family gatherings and celebrations. They spent very little time alone, however. There were always people around. Even so, the attraction they had for each other was obvious.

At one family gathering, during the course of the meal, one of the relatives jokingly said, "Hey, Emil, when are you and Erna going to get married? You've been going together for a long time."

Emil looked at Erna. "Yes, I guess we may as well set a date and get married."

Erna felt her face grow hot. What a marriage proposal! She knew he was shy, but this was ridiculous. What should she say? Everyone was staring at her, waiting for a reply. She really did want to marry him, but she had expected something a little more romantic, at least just the two of them together! In her heart, she knew if she said no he would never have the nerve to ask her again. Slowly she reached over and gave him a kiss.

"Why thank you for that proposal Emil. In front of everyone here, I accept. Since we have so many witnesses, your stuck with me!"

Everyone clapped and laughed. There was much cheering and whistling. Both Erna and Emil were embarrassed. Somehow they made it through the meal, sneaking shy looks at each other. After dinner came more congratulations. Erna began to think that maybe this wasn't so bad after all. Emil even put his arm around her—his grin spreading across his face.

Later, when they were alone, Emil asked: "When shall we get married?"

"When do you want to get married?"

"Well, I figure it may as well be right away. No sense waiting any length of time, the way I see it."

Erna's heart jumped. Things really were moving fast now. What should she say? Did she need more time?

"I do have to give notice at the hospital. I think they should have a month's notice at least, and I need time for wedding preparations."

Erna was stalling. She wasn't sure how much time she needed. "I would like to get married in church, and we have so many friends and relatives that would like to come." Her excitement was carrying her away as the words rushed out.

Emil frowned. He hadn't thought about all those things. All he had thought was that they could just go and get married. How could small plans suddenly grow into huge ones in the space of a few minutes?

"Well, what ever you think. I don't know too much about these things."

Erna sensed his hesitancy. Of course, he wouldn't really want all the fan fare that went with a wedding, while she thrived on such things. They sure were different! Guess they would just have to compromise and adjust to each other. It never crossed her mind that those difference could really create problems for them. She decided she may as well start adjusting right away.

"This is the middle of September, how does November the fifteenth sound to you? That would give me two months to make all the arrangements."

Emil gave her a squeeze. "Sounds just fine to me. November the fifteenth it shall be."

"Emil?"

"Yes?"

"Where will we live?"

"Well, I'm going to try to get us started on a farm of our own. If I don't make it in time we may have to stay with my parents for awhile, if that's okay with you?"

"Sure, that's okay." Erna was thrilled. A farm of their own! How wonderful! She could hardly wait. She loved farm life. "Let's go tell them." Erna grabbed his hand and started tugging.

"Tell who, what?"

"Everyone here. Let's tell them the date of our wedding." Erna was excited and happy.

"I guess—if you think so."

"Of course I think so silly, come on!"

Emil did not really want to be the center of attention again. He figured he'd had plenty for one day. But he didn't want to disappoint his 'bride to be' either, so he allowed himself to be pulled and tugged back into the main gathering. There Erna proudly announced their wedding date.

"My goodness, that really was fast. Emil, I didn't know you could move that fast," someone quipped.

"Guess he knows when he better move," said another.

Emil took it all in stride, smiling and not saying too much. As for Erna, she didn't mind the teasing, in fact, she quite enjoyed it all.

Back at the hospital, Erna announced her wedding day and, of course, her resignation to take effect within two months. Everyone was happy for her, but sad that she would be leaving them. Many expressed their sadness over her going, especially the matron.

Chapter 7

The Wedding

Anna shouted, "Erna! Erna! Where are you?" Anna's voice echoed up and down the hospital corridors.

Erna peeked out from a patient's room. "My goodness your noisy. I'm in here."

"Come quickly. I need you."

"You know better than that. I can't just walk away from a patient."

Anna sighed in exasperation. "Okay. I'll help you, then you must come with me, just for a few minutes. It's very important."

When the girls finished with the patient, Anna grabbed Erna's hand and fairly dragged her down the hallway.

"And I thought I could move fast. Come on, what's the hurry. Where are we going?"

Anna pulled her into the staff room where Erna was met with shouts of, "Surprise! Surprise!"

Erna stared around the room. Gathered there were nurses, doctors, cooks, cleaning staff, friends, and even some patients, including former patients who had become friends with Erna. Gifts were piled high on a table. Erna felt hot tears welling in her eyes.

"For me? Really, for me?"

"Yes Erna," confirmed the matron, "really for you. We're all going to miss you terribly." The matron gave Erna a hug and then escorted her to a chair of honor amid much applause.

That evening went by like a dream for Erna. Never had she felt so honored. She received many beautiful wedding gifts. She couldn't thank everyone enough. Anna agreed to drive Erna to Consort for the wedding. They could take all the gifts in the car. Erna didn't have a car, nor did she know how to drive.

As the wedding day approached, Erna frantically made arrangements. Many of the arrangements had to be make by her brother and his wife. Her niece, Bill's daughter, and one of Emil's sisters would be the bride's maids. They would make their own dresses so that Erna would just have to attend to her own. She asked Anna to go with her to find a dress and Anna agreed.

They drove to Calgary where Erna would have lots of choice. Searching through store after store, Erna tried on dozens of dresses but all were too big. Erna was just too small for what the stores carried.

"Aren't you getting tried Erna?" asked Anna in frustration.

"No. Are you?"

"Well, kind of. Seems you've tried enough on to be able to see you aren't going to find one to fit you."

"It's the only time in my life I'll ever get to try them on. They're so beautiful. But maybe you're right. I guess I'll just have to make my own."

Erna, tilting her head from side to side, was carefully examining a lacy, blue, floor length dress and picturing how she would look in it.

"You know," said Erna with mounting enthusiasm, "I really like this blue one. I could take a picture of it and make it. All I just have to do is find some blue material like that."

Anna examined the dress. "But Erna, you don't want to make your wedding gown in blue."

"Why not?"

"Brides wear white."

"But white is so drab, besides this blue is such a pale blue, it's nearly white, and I just love it." The words tumbled together as Erna tried to persuade Anna that blue would be the right color for her. In fact, the more Anna tried to discourage her, the more determined she became to make her dress exactly like the one she was looking at.

"Erna, it's tradition to wear white," insisted Anna

"Then I guess I'll be untraditional," responded Erna revealing her stubborn streak.

"It symbolizes," she hesitated then rushed on with her words as if determined to make this new Canadian understand, "It symbolizes that you are coming into your marriage a virgin."

Erna blushed, but her mind was set.

"I don't care," she answered defiantly, "I will have it in blue."

"What will Emil think?"

"I'm sure it won't make any difference to him."

In one last hopeless gesture her friend mumbled, "Maybe you won't be able to find the right material in blue."

But Erna did find the right material, and made her dress in a pale blue. She made one more trip to Calgary to get some fine pleating done. Everything else she did herself.

For years after her wedding Erna wore the dress in many community plays until someone washed it, instead of having it dry cleaned. The dress was ruined. Erna would shed many tears over the loss of her gorgeous wedding dress.

It was two days before her wedding. Erna had worked at the hospital as long as she could. She had hoped to get away earlier, but she had the responsibility of training her replacement who arrived later than expected. The matron, in desperation, imposed on Erna to stay a little longer. Erna reluctantly agreed. She phoned her brother and asked him to take care of last minute arrangements.

Snow had been falling for the last three days. Now a blizzard was forming. Erna had not paid much attention to the weather, but Anna, who would be driving her to Consort, had.

"It doesn't look good, Erna," said Anna with a frown. "We're getting a real storm out there."

"Oh, I'm not worried. Your a good driver."

"Thanks, but even good drivers can't get through plugged roads."

Erna paused. "Maybe we'd better get the car loaded and get out of here."

"I think so. Cut your good-byes short."

Within an hour the girls were on the road, but the storm was getting progressively worse. A knot of fear began to form inside Erna. The snow was deep and getting deeper. It swirled wildly making visibility almost zero.

They hadn't gone far when they noticed red flashing lights ahead. A blurry figure waved them to the side of the road.

"It's the police, Erna."

"I wonder what they want."

Anna rolled down the car window. The officer peered inside at the loaded car. "Looks like you girls are off on a long trip."

"We're heading to Consort."

"I'm sorry," said the officer, "but you'll have to turn back, the road is closed."

"What do you mean, the road is closed?" demanded Erna, her face turning pale.

"I mean the road is impassable. We're turning all traffic back."

"But I'm going to my wedding. You have to let us through," Erna said on the brink of tears.

"I'm sorry, Miss. You can continue if you insist, but you won't get through. The snow is just too deep."

"We have no choice, Erna, we have to go back," said Anna sadly.

Tears welled up in Erna's eyes and rolled down her cheeks.

"What will I do?"

"Well, Miss," said the officer, "I'm sure your fiance will wait for such a pretty girl."

"What about the guests. They'll be arriving. Everything is booked and waiting."

"Maybe your guests won't be getting through either," replied the officer.

Cautiously Anna turned the car around and headed back to High River, trying hard not to look at Erna, now sobbing uncontrollably. Once back, Erna threw herself onto Anna's bed and buried her face into the pillow. Anna placed a friendly arm around her.

"You know, Erna, maybe you should phone Emil."

"Yes, I guess that would be a good idea," replied Erna, trying to get hold of herself.

Emil appeared calm.

"It's okay Erna, don't cry. I knew you wouldn't be able to get through this storm. Take the next train to Coronation. It leaves the day after tomorrow. I will meet you there. I can't get out of here by car either. I will take the train from here and meet you there."

The phone was crackling and snapping from the storm, but Erna finally got the message straight.

"What about our wedding?" She began sobbing again.

"We'll have our wedding. Just don't worry about it. You just get here."

Erna didn't know how but Emil was so reassuring that she began to feel better.

Two days later, on what should have been her wedding day, she was on the train to Coronation. Anna promised to bring her gifts and belongings to her as soon as the storm let up and she could get through. All the good-byes had been said again and everyone tried to cheer her up. Her precious wedding dress went with her. After all, Emil promised her that she would have her wedding. The train chugged along slowly with a snow plow attached to the front of the engine. It didn't seem as though the train could go any slower without stopping.

It became the longest train ride Erna was ever to experience. The train got stuck and a reinforced plow was sent to help clear the track. Finally, after midnight on Nov. 18, 1935, Erna arrived at

Coronation. Emil was there, standing in the cold on the platform, waiting for her. She threw herself into his arms and cried.

"Oh Emil! oh Emil!"

He held her tight, trying to still her shaking body. "It's okay, honey. You're here, that's all that matters."

"What are we going to do now?"

"Well, I've been thinking it all out and this is what we're going to do. They are expecting us in Consort tomorrow, on this train." Emil eyed the train speculatively. "So we'll first book into the hotel and then we'll wake up the United Church minister and have him marry us. I got the license when I arrived here."

Erna's tears stopped and she looked at him in wonder.

"You're really serious?"

"Of course I'm serious. I never say anything I don't mean."

Through out their lives together, Erna found that statement to be true. She began to laugh, almost hysterically. "Emil, I just don't believe you!"

"Well believe me. I'm so sorry you can't have the fancy wedding you planned, but we're getting married, and that's that!"

"What about witnesses?"

"We'll find some even if we have to grab these train men here. After all, they're responsible for your getting here so late." He winked at her and grinned broadly. "Come on, let's get your belongings." He took her hand and pulled her along.

As if in a dream, Erna followed him. "Boy, that's going to be one shocked minister." She couldn't help herself, she began to giggle.

At the hotel, a surprised proprietor, eager to break the monotony of the long night ahead, happily agreed to wake his wife and accompany Erna and Emil to witnesses their marriage.

Erna couldn't contain her excitement.

"Can I wear my wedding dress? I brought it with me."

"Of course you can," replied Emil, giving her an enthusiastic hug.

By the time they were ready to go, the hotel manager had his car out and warmed up. A big, hastily hand-written sign was placed on the counter. It read: "Gone To A Wedding. Back Shortly!"

Holding her gown high to avoid the snow, Erna climbed into the car. At the Manse Emil trudged through deep snow to the house. A series of bangs on the door aroused a sleepy eyed minister. Upon hearing Emil's request, he became wide awake.

"Are you serious?"

Twice in one evening one of the most serious men on earth was being asked if he were serious.

"Yes sir. The reception will be waiting for us in Consort tomorrow and we have to be married by then. I have the license."

"I guess stranger things have happened. Bring your group in. I'll wake my wife and we'll get ready for a wedding!"

"My goodness, you even have a wedding dress." The minister stared at Erna as she came in. "Your looking too beautiful to be getting married in a Manse. You should be getting married in church."

Emil, sensing a flood coming, quickly said: "We were to be, but because of the storm we missed it."

Erna and Emil were married on November 18, 1935. Both were twenty-seven years old. Emil breathed a sigh of relief, while Erna cried as they held each other. No pictures were taken, but after returning home, they dressed in their wedding clothes and had a picture taken by their home on the farm.

Back at the hotel, a patiently waiting patron stared as the wedding troupe entered from the cold. An incredulous smile appeared on his face. He looked again at the sign on the counter. Yep. It was a wedding in the middle of the night. He wasn't seeing things. He shook his head as the nuptials sped up the stairs.

They were awakened a few hours later by the hotel manager shouting and banging on their door. "If you two don't get mobile, you'll will miss your train."

Rubbing her eyes, Erna awakened Emil and both hurriedly tumbled out of bed.

A headlong rush followed. There was no time for breakfast. In a mad dash, they just managed to climb aboard the train for Consort before it pulled out of the station. Emil had rearranged for John to hold the reception on this day. Would they miss that too? Erna found it very hard to sit still. She jumped around like a cat on a hot griddle! To calm her, Emil suggested they try to get a few minutes sleep before arriving in Consort.

"Sleep!" exclaimed Erna, "I'm much too excited to sleep. But you go ahead." After what seemed an eternity, they finally arrived at their destination.

At the Consort Station Erna's nephew, Ewald, waited for them in a covered sleigh and a pair of high stepping horses decorated with sleigh bells and colorful ribbons. Ewald shouted and waved at them. Erna ran to meet him. He welcomed her with a tremendous hug.

Erna felt proud and pampered as the sleigh took them to the reception. She and Ewald sang a few songs for old times sake. As many as could make it through the snow were gathered together waiting for the bride and groom, including those who were supposed to have been part of the wedding party. Erna put her wedding dress back on for everyone to see. She squealed with delight at the sight of a wedding cake that had been made for them.

"Oh look Emil, isn't it beautiful?"

Emil eyed the three tiered cake with skepticism. It did look beautiful, but what were the five babies sitting on the top of each layer for? They were indeed intricately made and probably took hours of work, but on a wedding cake?

"Why the babies, Erna?" asked Emil, "Is that some kind of hint? Fifteen of them yet?"

Erna laughed. "No silly, don't you know what the major news happening for this year has been?"

"No, I don't."

"The birth of the Dionne quintuplets. It's very exciting and unique. No one, that we can recall, has ever had five babies at once. And they're all alive!"

"So those are the quintuplets on our wedding cake?"

"Yep! Isn't that nice?"

Emil didn't exactly think so, but he wasn't going to spoil Erna's happiness, so he simply nodded his head.

In spite of the bad weather, the reception was excellently prepared. Though many guests were unable to attend, those who did made up for the missing ones in enthusiasm and enjoyment. Two silver cup holders had been purchased for the newly-weds in which to put their drinking cups. Erna expressed awe at the complex design of the sparkling silhouettes.

"Oh Emil, they're so beautiful. I've never seen anything like them."

"Neither have I. They're really lovely." This time Emil had no misgivings or doubts.

Erna and Emil spent the rest of the week in Consort, having a great time in spite of the snow and cold. It was a short-lived holiday that did nothing to prepare Erna for the trying days that would follow. Had it not been for her childhood experiences in Russia, she might not have been strong enough to endure the hardships that were to come.

Emil was born in Friedrichsfeld, Russia, a village much like the one in which Erna grew up. He with his mother and dad, Jacob, were on their way to Canada, in 1909. While in Liverpool, England, his mother, Elizabeth, fell after recently giving birth to Emil. The fall caused her to hemorrhage. She died later the same day. Jacob continued on to Canada, a single father with his infant son in his arms. Two years later he married Elizabeth's sister, Rosa Kary. Emil's aunt became his step-mother.

Jacob and Rosa went on to have nine children, four girls and four boys. One child died at birth. There were ten members of the family living at home when Emil brought his new wife to the homestead. One was an infant. Erna's life instantly became very complicated.

Jacob was a strict disciplinarian and ran his house with an iron hand. Perhaps under the circumstances, he had to. Perhaps, it came from his upbringing and the prevailing ideas of his generation. Perhaps it came from his army training in Russia. He took his training with Joseph Stalin. Jacob said that he left Russia because war was coming to Europe.

As the eldest son, Jacob had title to a large inheritance, plus all the tradition that goes with the background of the Maron name. His dad, realizing that Jacob was right and a war was coming, began to sell all his possessions and make preparations to follow his son to Canada. He was a very wealthy man. He held an auction that lasted for two days, with two auctioneers working full time. He sold the land separately. When all the arrangements for him and his family were made to set sail for Canada, the deal on the land fell through. He decided to go anyway after his relatives agreed to sell the land for him. In March 1913, he returned to Russia to get his money, only to find that the government had claimed it.

Jacob had developed his farm in Canada into a thriving enterprise. It produced grain, animal products and produce and was self-sustaining in everything but such items as coffee and sugar. All the children worked hard and Jacob had expected his oldest son, Emil, true to tradition, to stay on the farm and take it over from him. He was therefore not pleased to learn that Emil wanted his own place. Emil had not said anything about this situation to Erna, so she was about to find out the hard way. Perhaps he hadn't said anything in the hope that his dad would relent, take pity, and help him out. He was soon to learn that this was not to be.

The house was large, but not large enough to accommodate eleven people. Erna's first shock came when she learned that she would have to share a bedroom with Emil's parents! The room had been neatly divided in half by beautiful curtains, but that solved nothing as far as Erna was concerned.

"Emil, you mean this is your parent's room, they have the other half?"

"Yep." Emil smiled his usual happy smile.

"We don't get a room of our own?"

"Nope. They're all full up, and this is the largest room."

Erna stared at him. "But Emil, how can we — I mean how do you expect — I mean how are we going to have children with your parents right beside us?"

"Well, the usual way, I guess," replied Emil, his face flushing red.

"With your parents in the next bed?"

"I guess I never thought about that."

"Well you better start thinking about it!" Erna was angry and had Emil been the kind of person to argue, they would have experienced their first serious fight. "I sure hope, for your sake as well as mine, that we have our own place right soon!" Erna stormed out of the room.

If Emil would not argue with Erna, Jacob had no qualms against it. His and Erna's personality collided head on at every turn. Erna quickly settled in and became part of the industrious family. All immediately recognized Erna's kindliness, good will, love for all, and her willingness to work hard. But she would not give in to Jacob's stern rules and domination. He, on the other hand, felt she had to abide by his rules. He was head of this family and that was that! He tried in every way to dominate and belittle her. He frequently humiliated her in hopes that she would accept him as the authority. She hated the circumstances under which she lived but could not help admiring Jacob and his accomplishments.

One morning Jacob looked up menacingly from his breakfast and demanded, "Who cooked the porridge this morning?"

Everyone sat silently around the table, all eyes focused on Jacob. He slowly rose from the table.

Erna stood up too. Standing as tall as her small stature would allow, she looked him straight in the eye and answered. "I did."

She was positive that he knew she had cooked the porridge. He was baiting her.

Rosa, his wife, jumped up. "No Jacob, please don't."

"Quiet woman! Sit down!"

Quickly she turned and ran to the kitchen, tears filling her eyes.

"Dad, please," said Emil, who was now standing.

"When you cook porridge in this house, you make sure there are no lumps in it, understand?" He picked a lump out of his plate and threw it across the table. It landed in front of Erna.

Erna turned pale and felt sick to her stomach. How could he do such a thing? She was completely mortified! In spite of herself tears welled in her eyes and she ran to the room she shared with her tormentor. She threw herself on the bed and cried.

Emil followed her. He put his arms around her and whispered. "Forgive him Erna. He doesn't mean to be cruel, it's just his way."

"What do you mean he doesn't mean to be cruel? She sat up. Tears ran down her cheeks.

Emil pulled her close to him. "I'm sorry, I'm so sorry."

"You shouldn't have to apologize for him. I just can't take this any longer. When will we have our own place? Is he going to help us?"

Emil shook his head. "He wants us to stay here. He figures on me taking over this place, seeing how I'm the oldest son."

Erna stared at him in horror. "Oh no, oh please Emil, we can't stay here. We just can't!"

"Don't worry. We won't. Somehow, some way, we'll get our own place, with or without his help."

Comforted by his words, Erna clung tightly to him.

Perhaps it was this incident that brought Erna's temper to the boiling point. Her anger toward Jacob increased by the day. She abhorred the unfairness with which he treated his family and she felt he had to be told. She waited for her opportunity.

Jacob had a habit of getting everyone up at between four and five in the morning. After breakfast he expected everyone to go to work while he crawled back in bed for a couple more hours of sleep. No one else got that privilege and it annoyed Erna.

One day as he headed back to bed, Erna placed herself in front of him and asked:

"So what are your plans this morning, Jacob?"

"Is that a concern of yours?"

"Unfairness is."

"Are you implying that I'm unfair?"

"No, I'm not implying it, I'm saying it!"

By this time Rosa entered the scene. To avoid a conflict she took Erna's arm and tried to lead her away.

"No Erna, please, just leave him be."

"No, I won't. It's time he realized that being the head of a household doesn't give him the right to mistreat everyone."

"Oh, so you do acknowledge that I am the head of this household?" said Jacob sarcastically.

"I never said you weren't. But usually the head of an organization works harder then those under him. He doesn't go to bed after everyone else is working."

"Well, most certainly your head seems to be working this morning." Jacob was embarrassed at being confronted in this manner. No one had ever dared question what he did before and he was not quite sure how to handle the situation, especially since he knew that this little fire ball in front of him was right. Turning his back on her he stomped into the bedroom. But, try as he might, he could not sleep.

After a half hour of tossing and turning, he angrily jumped out of bed and marched to the kitchen where Erna was busy with the household chores. She flashed him a demure smile. He gave her a quick glance and stomped through the kitchen and out the door. Erna smirking. Served him right. He had it coming!

Later that day Emil asked Erna: "What did you say to dad this morning?"

"Why?" said Erna.

"Why? Because he told me I need to discipline that wife of mine and her bitter tongue, that's why."

So she had a bitter tongue, did she? "I didn't say much," said Erna with a shrug.

"Just what did you say?" Emil demanded.

"I told him that I didn't think he was treating everyone fairly."

"You said that?" Emil was appalled.

"Well, he really isn't being fair!" Erna insisted.

Emil also thought his dad was unjust, but he was a good manager and Emil would never have spoken against him. He stared at Erna and wondered what kind of a wife he had? Maybe he didn't know her as well as he thought he had. She certainly had courage. He gave her a hug. "Don't worry about it, let it pass. Guess we'll just let it slide and see what happens."

Erna wasn't too sure she knew what he meant, but she thought it best she not ask. From then on Jacob ignored her. Unless she spoke directly to him, he treated her as if she didn't exist. This kind of relationship was very hard for Erna. It was like he knew what hurt her the most. You couldn't fight back if you were ignored. Erna cried and complained to Emil. She insisted that they have their own place!

That winter was long and hard. Erna felt bleak, dreary and cheerless as signs of spring began to appear. It was then that Emil came back, from a trip to town. He carried his typical smile on his face.

"Why are you so happy?" asked Erna.

"I have some news for you."

"If it's good news, I can sure use it."

Emil dragged her off to a private corner of the house. "There's this little farm about four miles from here. The owner has a store in town and no longer wants to farm. He is willing to rent it to us."

Erna stared at him. "You mean a place of our own?"

"That's what I mean."

"Oh, Emil, yes, yes, yes.!" She threw her arms around him.

"Hold it. Not so fast. There are some problems."

"I don't care about the problems. We'll work them out, just as long as we have our own place."

"You might care about this one. The house has only one room and a dirt floor."

"We can build a floor and add to the house, can't we?" Erna was ready to go right then.

"I guess we can," said Emil. But he wondered how much they should put into a place that wouldn't be their own.

They rented the Hamilton farm. Happily Erna ordered furniture through the Sears Catalogue. She agreed to pay for it out of the savings she had accumulated while working. She also had cattle that she had bought. They were on her brother Bill's farm.

Emil's brothers, Sam and Oscar, both good carpenters, helped put in a floor. Sam also made a small ornamental table for Erna on which to place trinkets. It was about three feet long, a foot wide and stood about three feet high. It's still in the family today. It served as a wedding gift to Erna.

The furniture arrived before anticipated. Jacob happened to be in town the day it came and was asked to pay the freight on it. Reluctantly he did. Back home he handed the bill to Erna.

"Here, paid for. That's your wedding gift."

Meekly Erna took the bill. "Thank you, Sir."

Jacob also gave Emil some much needed farm machinery to help him get started, but Canada was in the throes of the Great Depression and making a living off the farm would not be easy. But Erna and Emil held on to each other and vowed they would make a go of it in spite of the depression. Together they put in their first crop in the spring of 1936.

Chapter 8

Farming Or Dusting?

1936 - the middle of the worst depression Canada has ever known, now remembered as 'the dirty thirties.' This was Erna and Emil's first year of farming. Did they realize it was a depression? To some extent they did, but little did they understand just how bad it could really be. They only knew that they would work to make a go of it, and they would, no matter what! Everywhere farms were going under, people were leaving. Some men were forced to leave their families in search of work, sometimes just for meals. One less at home meant one less mouth to feed.

In towns women set out kettles of soup to feed unemployed men as they tumbled off the train looking for work. The soup was made from what little they had produced from dirt dry gardens. There was no rain. Everything dried up and the top soil blew away. The rail riders had no money. They jumped on the train while in motion and jumped off before it stopped—a tricky business indeed. Some never made it. Often they slept outside. Occasionally a kind soul might take them in for the night in return for labour. If they could scrape together a few pennies, they might share a hotel room with six or seven other men.

Animals starved where they once grazed in lush fields. There was little water. Even the grass withered. No wonder Mr. Hamilton decided to rent out his farm.

Erna and Emil worked to exhaustion every day. In frustration Erna would cry, "What are we going to do? The animals are getting so thin. We have no flour left. And this dust, I just can't stand this dust anymore. It's just too horrible!"

Emil wrapped her in his strong arms, but he could offer no solutions.

"I cover up the bed," continued Erna, "I have to wash dishes before we can even use a cup. We eat and breathe dirt. Now the broom is so worn, I can hardly sweep with it anymore."

Emil looked out the window. He could barely see across the yard for dust. Banks of dirt drifted like snow. "I think maybe we should sell that one big steer out there so we can buy a few things," said Emil.

"But we were going to have him for meat ourselves."

"We'll just have to butcher one of the others for the winter. We have nothing to feed them anyway."

"I suppose your right." Erna shivered as she gained comfort from the strong arms around her.

They sold the steer. Emil came home bearing devastation on his face.

"What's wrong, Emil? Didn't the steer sell?" asked Erna.

"He sold, but I only got eight dollars for him."

"Eight dollars? That's all? Now what are we going to do?"

"Guess we'll buy a broom and what ever else we can get for eight dollars."

Christmas was coming, but there was no money for gifts or celebrations, but Erna carried a special Christmas surprise for Emil. She was pregnant. Emil was elated.

Seeing the happiness on Emil's face brought joy to Erna in an otherwise dreary setting. She had been worried that he might not want a baby, because of the difficult times they were experiencing. Together they spread the news to family and friends. All rejoiced with them.

As spring arrived the land remained barren and dry. There appeared to be no hope that their second year of farming would be any different than their first. Then Jacob called on Emil to come see him. He had a special project he wanted to discuss. Erna was disgusted. It seemed as though Emil's dad still felt his oldest son was working for him and could be at his beck and call whenever he wished. When Emil returned home he wore a broad smile.

"Must have been a good meeting. You look like the cat that caught the canary."

"Honey, I really think dad's got something this time. Sit down I'll tell you about it."

Erna sat down and listened.

"Well, him and the boys are building a water well digging machine."

"A what machine?" Erna interjected.

"A machine that drills for water. He figures, things being like they are, there is a great need for water. He wants me to go drilling wells with him. I could make enough money to tide us over until the farming improves."

Erna thought awhile.

"We could sure use the money. But what about our farm? How can you do both? And do you think anyone has any money to pay for wells?"

"I guess we'll just have to pray that there are some people who can pay for wells. As for our farm, don't look like it's going to make much sense to put crops in anyway. I'll just put in what I can in between drilling."

"Maybe I can put some in myself." Erna was catching his enthusiasm.

"No your not. Remember your having a baby," protested Emil.

"Don't worry. I'm strong, and I'll have a strong baby." Erna laughed and patted her stomach.

The drilling machine was a success. Emil and Jacob accumulated more business than they could handle, some from far away. Their success kept Emil away from home more than he had anticipated. Erna worried about the farm. She put in a garden and as much of the crop as she could. She drove a pair of oxen, neighbours joked, better than Emil. She milked cows, and fed all the live stock. At the end of each long day she wearily collapsed into bed. Emil worried about her, but there was nothing much he could do about it. They desperately needed the money he made from drilling. Sometimes he was paid in poultry or other live stock which also required feeding, or butchering and canning. More work for Erna.

As time for the baby's arrival drew near, Emil refused to go drilling with his father. Jacob was angry, of course, but Emil stood up to him and returned home to be by his wife's side. Had he not, Erna may not have survived the birth.

In the middle of the night Erna awakened Emil. "I think it's time," she said.

"Time for what?" groaned Emil.

"For the baby to come. I think we better get to the hospital."

Emil jumped out of bed.

"Isn't it a bit early?"

"Well sometimes babies come early. They don't always come on the appointed days."

It was forty miles to the hospital in Consort. Those forty miles seemed like forever to Erna whose pains progressively increased in intensity. But she was happy and sang all the way.

At the hospital, Emil seldom left Erna's side. Two days after she was admitted, she was taken to the delivery room. Emil was not allowed to accompany her and was thus spared some frightful moments.

Erna's labor was difficult and the pain almost unendurable.

"Hang tight Erna," commanded the nurse who was holding her hand. "Your baby is turned sideways. We're going to try and turn it."

Gentle hands pushed and prodded and slowly turned the baby. The doctor administered an anesthetic to help relieve the pain and stop the labor pangs. Whenever the baby was maneuvered into the correct position, it would slip into its former position. Erna became exhausted. Today, doctors would perform a c-section under similar circumstances.

In desperation the doctor approached Emil nervously pacing in the waiting room and said, "I don't know how to tell you this, but we have no choice but to take your babies life. If we don't, your wife will die."

Tears entered Emil's eyes. "You know what's best, doctor," he said with trembling voice. "Do what you have to."

The baby was born dead, the cord wrapped around its neck. Erna remained in serious condition. It was decided not to tell her about the baby until she could regain some strength. The doctor feared for her life.

While Erna was recovering, Emil, with relatives and friends, buried the baby in a little cemetery close to home. He would always wonder if the death might have been his fault. Would things have been different had he stayed home and put in the crops and looked after the farm so Erna would not have had to do so much physical labor?

Erna's strength began to return. She continually asked for her baby, but her pleas were always met with excuses of why she couldn't see the baby. Then one day she insisted. The nurse told her:

"Your husband and the doctor will be here later. They will talk to you."

"But why can't you bring my baby? Is it a girl or a boy?

"A girl."

Erna smiled. "Please, I want to see her."

The nurse hurried out of the room without answering. This was Erna's first inkling that something was wrong. Several hours later Emil and the doctor entered her room.

Erna sat up, grimacing with pain.

"Emil, what's wrong? They won't bring me our baby."

Emil put his arm around her. The doctor pulled a chair up beside the bed.

"Mrs. Maron, I'm, afraid I have bad news for you."

"What's the matter? What's wrong with our baby? She's alive, isn't she?"

"Your baby didn't make it, Mrs. Maron."

Erna buried her face in Emil's shoulder.

"But why? Why? What happened?"

Emil held her tight. "They had to take the baby's life, honey, or you would have died."

The doctor quietly left while Emil wiped away her tears.

"We'll have another baby, Erna. God will grant us another," continued Emil.

"Can I see her?"

"Erna, you've been out of it for several days. The baby was buried."

"Oh."

"I'm sorry. I didn't know what else to do."

"That's okay." There was silence. "Did she have any hair?"

Emil smiled. "She was beautiful, just like you. And she did have hair. Piles of it, dark black hair." Another pause. "You know, we have all these papers to fill out. We have to give her a name."

Erna hesitated, then asked: "What do you want to name her?"

"Well, I thought you should name her."

The baby was named Marina. It was August, 1937. Erna remained in the hospital awhile longer and then was allowed to go home.

Once home, Erna suggested they start adding on to their little house. She felt they both needed something to take their minds off the baby. Emil was reluctant. It wasn't their place, and might never be.

"Do you really think we should? asked Emil. "We might get the house all built up and then have to leave."

"But, then again, it could become our own place, and we really need the extra space," insisted Erna.

"I suppose your right." Emil gave in. Perhaps he sensed Erna's need for diversion at this time. Perhaps he needed diversion as well. With Sam's and Oscar's help two bedrooms, a large living room and kitchen were added along with a little porch off the kitchen. Erna was pleased. Eagerly she worked along side the men, finishing the inside of the house.

In 1939, Erna was again expecting. Her past experience caused her some worry. What if something happened to this baby too? Rumors of a Second World War added to her fears. Oscar, eager for adventure, enlisted in the army. Everywhere men were volunteering for military service, some for no better reason than the army would supply them with food and clothing.

The war did create jobs and brought an end to the depression with the ever increasing need for war materials.

A great feeling of unease fell over Erna and she expressed her unease to Emil.

"What if you're called to war like the men in Russia were? I just can't believe another war is coming — that we should have to live through this another time."

"Don't worry," assured Emil, "the war is on the other side of the ocean. Your in Canada now. It won't be the same."

"But I'd just die if you had to go. And what about our baby. How could I have it alone? Something might happen again."

Emil gathered her in his arms. "It will be okay. I won't have to go. Canada doesn't have conscription."

"That could change."

"I don't believe so. Not here. We live in a free country."

August 8, 1939, exactly two years after the loss of her first baby, Erna gave birth to another girl. She was named Ruby after a little girl Erna had once taken care of.

"Emil, look at her black hair." Emil eyed the tousled haired baby girl in Erna's arms and the love of his family showed on his face.

On September 1, 1939, Germany invaded Poland. Two days later Britain declared war on Germany. On September 10, Canada and France joined Britain to declare war on Germany. World War II had begun, thrusting the planet in turmoil. It would last six long years. Forty-two thousand Canadians would die defending Canada's freedom.

Emil didn't have to go to war. He and Erna continued to work hard to improve their little farm and, with the rise in grain prices due to the war, it began to produce a living for them.

In June of 1942, Erna and Emil were blessed with another baby girl. This one had very little hair. What she did have was blond. They named her Carol, meaning a song of praise and joy. Erna felt supreme happiness and sang most of the time.

Many other Canadians experienced no such joy. In August about 5,000 Canadians attacked the French Port of Dieppe in a disastrous raid. More than 3,000 were killed, wounded, or taken prisoner by the Germans. But two months later the Germans were defeated in the Battle of El Alamein and began a retreat across North Africa.

One year later, July, 1943, Erna and Emil had a third baby girl. They named her Linda after Erna's brother John's oldest girl whom Erna had practically raised after the death of John's first wife. The two Lindas would be called little Linda and big Linda.

Erna's happiness was dimmed when her doctor informed her that she could not have any more babies. Being so small and having worked so hard caused her much difficulty in child bearing. Her sorrow was mostly for Emil, for now he would never have a son.

Emil smiled. "It doesn't matter. Just look at the wonderful girls I have."

"Are you sure?" She raised worried eyes to his face.

"Of course I'm sure. Don't be silly and worry over such a thing."

"But there will be no son to help you with the farm."

"I guess we will just have to put our girls to work. After all, look what you can accomplish, and your a girl."

Erna smiled. Yes, she thought, maybe the girls would be better farmers than boys. She would do everything in her power to teach them.

In September, 1944, Canadian troops captured Dieppe, France, the place where they had formerly suffered such great losses. All across allied lines the enemy retreated. World War II was fast winding down. On April 30, 1945, Hitler, committed suicide. Seven days later Germany surrendered. Three months later the Americans dropped two atomic bombs on Japan, forcing it to surrender. World War II officially ended.

Everywhere people rejoiced and celebrated as they waited for friends and relatives to return home. Emil's brother, Oscar, amid great shouts of gladness, returned home. He would never be the same as when he left to fight for his country. He appeared moody and sullen. His behavior was unpredictable, and he experienced frequent nightmares. Erna's and Emil's hearts went out to this ambitious boy who had returned too them a broken man. Once again Erna witnessed the bizarre results of war.

The influx of returning men, many with wives they married overseas, caused a boom in the farming sector. New farms sprung up across the country. Grain was being grown everywhere. Grain required harvesting. Many new farmers had no means and no idea of how to get their crops harvested. The amount of acreage seeded was more than could be harvested before winter set in. Erna and Emil, themselves, had begun to seed more land as the markets increased. An emergency community meeting was called to try to deal with the situation.

A volunteer spokesman set the mood of the meeting.

"The way I see it," he said "we have to all work as a team. Maybe we can go in together and buy a threshing machine that will speed up harvesting. Seems they can put out a lot of grain in a big hurry."

The murmuring of assent prompted the spokesman to ask for a show of hands in favour, but one frantically waving hand halted the process.

"Wait, just a minute. Seems to me we need more discussion first. Who would be waiting until last to get his crops off? Maybe things will take longer than you think and someone might be left stuck for the winter."

Complete silence ensued as the idea was digested. None wanted to be last.

"Any suggestions? asked the spokesman. Silence. "I suggest," he continued, "that the one who is last this year be first next year."

Smiles and nodding of heads followed his suggestion.

"Any volunteers to be last this first year?"

Silence. Not getting a crop off could lead to a desperate winter. Emil shuffled his feet uncomfortably. Finally he put his hand up. Erna poked him and gave him a dirty look.

"Yes! Yes! We have a volunteer. Emil has just volunteered to be last on this new, grand community venture."

Everyone applauded Emil who smiled and blushed. Dismayed, Erna saw no occasion to clap and cheer.

The new threshing machine would be purchased. Next, a hat containing numbers was passed around to determine the order in which the land would be harvested. This brought about a heated discussion on the possibility that the one first on the list may not have a crop ripe enough to take off first. It was then agreed that he be moved one down the list, until his crop was ready.

All returned home satisfied with the results, except Erna.

"Why did you do that?" she demanded.

"Well, somebody had to or the whole project would have fallen through, and that would have been even worse."

"I suppose your right. But why you?"

"Didn't seem like anyone else was going to."

"They could have drawn numbers for that too."

"I suppose so, but it probably would have been voted down before they got to that point."

In her mind Erna thought that he was likely right. That group had to have some kind of a push to encourage them on any new idea, especially one involving money. She said nothing more. She just hoped that everyone would come up with their share of the money for the machine.

The threshing machine was purchased just before harvest time. It went to the first farmer on the list. The whole community, as well as curious others from great distances, gathered to watch its first operation.

They hauled the bundled grain to the machine in large wagons piled high, and pulled by teams of two horses. Every farmer involved provided a wagon and team. True to claims, the machine greedily gobbled up the grain as fast as the men could bring it in and pitch it from the wagons into its monstrous mouth. The fresh, clean harvested grain was then spit out into another wagon, belonging to the owner of the field. It was then hauled to the granary. Some was sold immediately, some kept until a future sale date, and some was kept for livestock. A huge stack of straw spewed from another part of the machine. The farmer would use this as winter bedding for his animals.

Everyone was amazed by what this machine could accomplish in such a short time. Joyful farmers moved from one field to another, from one farm to another, with much enthusiasm, laughter, and joking, in spite of the hard grueling work and long hours they had to endure.

The weather started turning cold when the machine at last came to Emil's farm. Both he and Erna were thrilled and excited. Erna had been baking and cooking for the past two weeks, preparing for the crew that would be arriving. This was no easy task with three small children plus farming chores to do, as Emil had been away from early morning till late at night threshing on other farms.

At 4:00 in the morning she leaped out of bed, humming to herself as she quickly moved around. Then she stopped and listened. What was that she heard?

"Emil?"

"Yep?"

"I hear something in the yard."

"Oh my goodness. Someone must be here already." Emil ran out the door only to return a few minutes later with a couple of men in tow.

"Any coffee ready?" said Emil. "These guys are here already."

"Just about. You men must have left home in the middle of the night."

Erna frantically dumped coal into the large cook stove. A smaller wood and coal burning stove occupied part of the living room, keeping the house cozy warm. The living room was where Erna had set up a number of make-shift tables to feed the crew that would be arriving.

"Couldn't sleep anyway," said one of the men. "Thought we may as well get this show on the road. Last place, don't want the snow to hit."

The men, also, were excited, knowing that the community decision had been the right one and that working together had certainly paid off.

By 6:00 a.m. threshing was in full swing. Four hours later they shut down for breakfast. At 2:00 in the afternoon they stopped for dinner. Supper was served at 7:00 that night. The crew then continued to work until after 11:00 p.m. before heading home. The teams of horse wagons remained at the farm until the harvesting was complete.

Erna was a wonderful cook and the men thoroughly enjoyed her meals. They expressed as much in their comments.

Erna beamed, noticing one man's plate piled as high with food as possible with a wedge of pie topping the whole thing. Good grief! What stomachs they must have!" Erna shuttered.

Over the years the community would continue to work together to harvest their crops. Many problems would arise, but they were always worked out. Some with much noise, flaring tempers and arguments. Erna and Emil stood strong, as solid bricks, uniting and helping their community. Should a neighbour be in trouble or in need, they would always be there, ready and willing to do what they could.

Another important example of community spirit was Erna's telephone work. With her love for people Erna could not stand to be isolated. She had installed not one but two phones. A main line ran from pole to pole across the country along side the road. Another ran along barbed wire fences that enclosed grazing land. Those who could not afford to join the main line connected themselves to the barbed wire line.

The phones were huge, heavy, oblong boxes nailed to a wall in the house. A crank on one side of the box was turned to call out. Every telephone owner had their own ringing signal as more than one party could be on the line at the same time. Erna and Emil had their phone on the living room wall and their barbed wire phone on the kitchen wall. This enabled Erna to know which phone was ringing. Her signal to answer the main line was one long ring followed by three short ones. Her signal to answer the barbed wire phone was four short rings. Pasted on the wall beside the phones were the signals for friends and acquaintances connected to those lines.

Before long news spread that Erna and Emil had two phones. As a result, Erna inadvertently became something of a 'switch board operator.'

People would call on one line and ask Erna to call someone on another and relay a message.

Erna would listen with great care to every request, discussing the pros and cons of the situation, and perhaps offering some advice. She would then go to the other phone to pass on the message with, perhaps, a little extra advice. She kept herself busy in this way while enjoying herself at the same time. She knew what was happening on every farm and in every household in the community, and, in some cases, in surrounding communities and towns. Anyone having a question about something or someone in the community would just phone Erna and ask her. She usually had an answer.

Some of the messages she received should have been given, by the person calling, in person, but Erna would dutifully abide by all wishes.

A conversation might go something like this:

"Hi Erna!"

"Hi!"

"I have a very important message. Do you suppose you could transfer it?"

"Sure. What's the message?"

"Tell so-and-so I love her."

Silence.

"Erna?"

"Yes?"

"Are you still there? Did you get it?"

"Yes, I got it, but shouldn't you tell her yourself?"

"Can't get to her."

"I think that's a pretty poor excuse."

"Will you pass on the message?"

Erna gave a very audible sigh. "Yes, I guess so."

"Thanks Erna. Let me know what the reply is, will ya!"

The most important role Erna played in her telephone message center occurred during a large prairie fire.

Mrs. Myers, Erna's friend and neighbor, came on the line. Erna could tell by the sound of Mrs. Myers voice that it was an urgent call.

"There's a terrible grass fire about sixty miles to the south!" she exclaimed, fighting to catch her breath. "We need all the men and equipment we can get as fast as possible. Tractors and plows, cats, trucks, water, heavy wet rags, anything for fighting it. It's going real good Erna, and in this wind there's no telling how far it'll go."

"I'll get right on it."

"I'll keep in touch, Erna, and let you know where to send the men and equipment."

"Okay."

Erna ran out in the yard to tell Emil. She knew he would want to go. She also knew how fast a prairie fire could spread, devastating everything in its path. They might themselves be burned out!

As Emil made preparations to go, she hurried back to the other phone. She dialed one long continuous ring. This meant emergency, and everyone on the line was expected to answer the phone.

"Emergency, emergency," repeated Erna. "All men and equipment for fire fighting needed south, as fast as possible. I will ring back shortly to give instructions where to go."

A few answered, but she knew there were a lot more that had got the message already. No sooner had she hung up when the main phone rang again. It was the original caller with dispatch instructions for men and equipment. Tractors with plows were to meet in three different areas to plow main fire guards depending on where the farmer lived. Most farmers, including Emil, already had fire guards plowed around their buildings. Those that didn't were to do so immediately. If the fire jumped the first main guard, perhaps it could be stopped at the second, etc. Emil would be at the last and final guard with his tractor and plow. The rest of the men and equipment were to go straight to the fire and try and stop it.

Erna relayed the instructions with another emergency ring. Emil hugged her and the girls and left as fast as his tractor would travel. He would be the first to start the final fire guard.

All day long Erna ran from one phone to the other with messages, instructions, and news of the fire. By evening she could see a big, black, cloud of smoke billowing on the horizon to the south. She knew that two farmers had been completely burned out and that the fire had jumped both the first and second fire guards and was now heading for the third and final one where Emil was stationed. She also knew that one tractor and plow had been lost to the fire.

The farmer escaped the flames when a truck came to his aid and carried him to safety.

Then Erna received the order to stand by to evacuate. She packed the car and turned all the animals loose. There was nothing more she could do for them. The phones kept ringing. She asked everyone to please stay off the lines so she could send the evacuation message. It never came.

Joyfully Erna would get to announce that the fire had been halted at the third fire guard. Enough men and equipment had been mustered to widen the guard and bring the advancing fire to a halt.

Emil arrived home early in the morning, tired, dirty, and covered with soot. It didn't matter. Erna and Emil embraced each other, thankful that the crisis was over. Together they gave thanks to God.

Chapter 9

Children and Family

In 1947 Mr. Hamilton died. His daughter Edith inherited the farm and continued to rent it to Erna and Emil.

Erna and Emil enrolled their eldest daughter, Ruby, in school for the first time. Because the little white school was several miles away, Emil had to drive his budding scholar there every morning and pick her up at the end of the school day. This took a lot of time away from his farming. It seemed as if he'd no sooner get started at something when he'd have to hurry off to pick up Ruby. It became very inconvenient.

Then Erna suggested that they buy the neighbor's shetland pony that had a habit of crawling through the fence to be with their horses. Ruby could ride the pony to school.

Emil was skeptical. "Ride that jumpy little thing?" he said. "She don't even know how to ride."

"She'd learn." insisted Erna. "I was riding when I was her age."

Emil looked dubious, but interested. It certainly would save time, and Erna was usually right about matters like this.

"Maybe it would be worth a try," thought Emil.

It turned out that the neighbor was very glad to sell the pony since he couldn't keep her home anyway. It became the ideal solution for all concerned. The pony came with the handle Montgomery which was reduced to Monty.

With Erna's instructions, Ruby was soon riding like an expert. With an air of independence and pride, she rode to school each day, saving her dad a lot of time and trouble. Erna was happy with her success and Emil felt liberated with the extra time he now had.

Then came winter in all its fury. Snow piled up in huge drifts and Emil was again driving Ruby to school with horses and sleigh. When the weather improved Monty was pressed back into service.

But after having enjoyed a period of leisure, she felt no great inclination to return to her former duties.

From the kitchen window, Erna watched Ruby struggling with Monty at the end of the lane. Monty stood stubbornly shaking her head and bracing her front hooves while kicking up the back ones. Ruby could do nothing with her. Angrily, Erna stomped out of the house and down the lane.

"Get off!" ordered Erna. "I'll show you how to make her move!"

With one leap Erna landed on the pony's back. In the same instant Monty kicked up her back end in the orneriest buck she could muster. Erna flew head first into a large snow bank. All her experiences with horses and mules hadn't prepared her for this testy little shetland.

Fuming and sputtering, Erna hauled herself out of the snow bank as Emil approached. Trying desperately but unsuccessfully to conceal his typical grin, he grabbed the pony's reins and said "I'll take Ruby to school with the team today." He then led the pony away.

Spitting and sputtering, Erna marched back up the lane to the house, vowing that Monty would definitely not get away with this! She would show her who was boss around this place. She would go when she was supposed to go and do what she was supposed to do, and that was that!

Many more confrontations followed. But in the end Monty carried the girls back and forth to school, day after day, year after year, by one means or another.

Maintaining miles of barb wire fencing required on prairie farms was and still is a tough job. Cattle and horses felt no compulsion to be enclosed behind wires, especially when grass was always greener on the other side. Many fences were continually kept in a state of disarray and Emil's were no exception.

One day the three girls ran into the house yelling, "Mom, mom!"

"Don't shout. I can hear you."

"There's some cows in the garden again! They're eating up the pea plants! Hurry mom!"

"Couldn't you have chased them out?" said Erna in exasperation.

"We tried. They just jump away from us and start eating another pea plant."

Fuming in frustration, Erna grabbed the broom from behind the door and ran down the lane toward the garden. Three of the felons were enjoying the lush vegetation when out of the corners of their eyes they spotted trouble coming at break neck speed. Up went their tails and away they went. Erna knew she couldn't run as fast as they could, so she threw the broom after them.

"Scat, get out of here! Next time I'll get you, you miserable cowardly cows!"

But the fun wasn't over. When the cows started to run, the dog took after them, barking and yelping, trying his best to aid Erna in the chase. At full tilt the cows zoomed back through the fence and into the pasture, taking a lot of the fence down with them.

The horses were also in the pasture. Monty watched the commotion, standing head high, hooves prancing. What right did that dog have chasing those cows anyway? She didn't like the dog at the best of times. He had tried to chase her too on many occasions. She'd fix this intruder. Head down she lunged at the dog and bit him on the back. Yelping with pain and surprise the dog zoomed toward Erna for protection. Erna's girls stood rooted in their tracks watching the bedlam unfold and marveling on the bazaar things that could happen when their mother became involved.

Erna turned and spotted them gawking at her.

"What are you three staring at? Get, back to the house!"

They did as told, but they couldn't wait to spill this story to their dad when he came in from the field that night, much to Erna's disgust. The whole family laughed uproariously over the affair. The next day found the entire family out trying to repair the frazzled fence.

With Emil spending the greater part of his time in the fields, disciplining the girls fell on Erna's shoulders. This was especially true during the summer months. She handled the job with great expertise and imagination.

The girls all had specific chores. One of Ruby's included letting the chickens out of their house first thing in the morning and feeding them. One morning Erna told Ruby not to let the chickens out because she wanted to catch and butcher one for supper. Feeling sorry for the chickens, Ruby deliberately let them out.

When Erna saw what Ruby had done, she cried, "Ruby! Come here at once!"

Slowly Ruby appeared around the door.

"Didn't I tell you not to let the chickens out this morning?"

No answer.

"Well, didn't I?"

"Yes."

"So why did you?"

Again no answer.

"I am going to have to spank you for not listening to what you are told. You know we have to eat. You know there's a reason for things your told to do and things your told not to do. You haven't been listening very well lately . I have no choice but to punish you."

As she reached for Ruby, Ruby bolted out the door and ran toward the barn and around the hay stacks, her heart pounding. She didn't think she should be punished for trying to save those poor chickens. It just wasn't fair!

As her emotions cooled, the truth of what she had done struck her. She had run away from her mom! She could be coming to get her at this very moment! Then she would get much worse than a spanking. Her mind began calculating the cost of what she had done and what could be worse than a spanking. Maybe she would be left home alone the next time the family went on an outing. She peeked around the hay stack. No sign of mom.

Ruby decided to stay where she was until dad got home and appeal to him for clemency. Maybe she could dig a hole in the side of the stack and hide there just in case mom was still looking for her.

Content with her plans, she skipped around another stack and, BANG, ran smack into her mother, who grabbed her with a grip that meant business. Ruby's mouth fell open. How on earth did she get around that stack so fast? It was the furthest one away. how could she run that fast!

Ruby had sorely miscalculated her mother's capabilities and things didn't look good for her.

She got her spanking as promised, and, for running away, she was confined to her bedroom for the rest of the day. She was allowed out for lunch and supper. What was worse, all her tears did not swing dad to her side. When he got home, he strongly suggested that in the future she had better listen to her mother. Then he gave her a gentle hug to somewhat ease her pain.

Whenever possible, Erna made Sunday a special day of joy and honor to God. So much so that the family attended three different churches of three different denominations every Sunday.

Erna greeted each Sunday with much enthusiasm and could be heard sharply delivering commands to Emil and the girls, "Hurry up Emil! Move it girls! We're going to be late."

The girls would scurry about, but Emil, undisturbed as always, would just smile and teasingly assure her, "I'm sure everyone will wait for you."

Erna would always try on a look of contempt but only manage to produce a diffident smile. He probably was right. The United Church minister knew personally everyone who came to his services. He knew who would be sure to be there and who wouldn't. The small congregation gathered at the town hall in nearby Hemaruka. After the service members of the congregation would enjoy visiting with each other before returning home.

Later in the afternoon the family would attend the little white community Lutheran Church. One Sunday their preparations were interrupted by a vehicle pulling into the yard.

"Oh no!" exclaimed Erna. "We have company! Emil, quick see what they want."

As he walked past her, Emil patted her shoulder. "Calm down, we'll make it okay."

"I suppose your going to say they'll wait for us too?"

"They probably will." He grinned as he went out the door. He returned shortly. "Don't worry. They just asked for directions in this 'forsaken land', as they called it."

"Don't seem very forsaken around here."

"Nope. Lots of energy being radiated around here."

They arrived at church on time and were warmly greeted. After service visiting again took place before heading home. Erna whipped up an appetizing supper and evening farm chores were done.

"Hurry up Emil! Move it girls! Church starts at seven. We're going to be late."

This time they were off to the Pentecostal Church at Veteran, Alberta, about twenty-five miles away. This church had a much larger congregation. Visiting after the service was cut to a minimum as they had to get the girls home and into bed. There was school the next day. This routine was followed each wonderful Sunday.

Erna and her family lived in a friendly and active community. The town hall provided a gathering place for the many events sponsored by the community. Most of the events included entertainment. This encouraged Erna to teach her girls to sing. Ruby, being the oldest, received guitar and piano lessons. The girls were soon performing in church and at community events, making their parents were very proud of them. There was, however, one problem. Accomplishments require work. Music requires lots of practice, especially for the amount of singing the girls were expected to do. Like most children, they tired of it all and sometimes rebelled.

On one occasion Erna called the girls to practice singing. They decided to make a quick exit and find a peaceful place to hide until practice time was over.

"I'm getting so tired of practicing all the time," said Ruby.

"Me too," echoed her sisters. "Why do we have to sing all the time anyway? Other kids don't."

"If we miss practice we won't have to sing," said Carol hopefully. Ruby, somewhat reluctant to defy her mother, remembering her past experience, said, "Maybe we should just go and get it over with."

"No! I'm not practicing!" insisted Carol. "Let's go hide in the barn. We'll Circle around the machinery so she doesn't see us."

Two of them scampered away, leaving Ruby behind. With a big sigh, Ruby decided to follow the others. Once inside the barn they listening intently. They could still hear their mother calling them.

"We're going to really get it for this, you know," said Ruby.

"No we won't," replied Carol. "She won't know we even heard her. She'll think we were playing where we couldn't hear her calling."

As they argued, they heard Erna's voice right outside the barn.

"Girls!"

The girls stared at each other. Then, they made a 'bee-line' to a manger and hid. They could hear Erna walking back toward the house. For about a half hour they sat scrunched up in the manger, hardly breathing and not daring to move. Suddenly, there was a rustling above them. They all looked up at a square black hole, used for pitching down hay to feed the animals. The rustling continued. The hole looked dark and foreboding. The girls moved a little closer to each other, as if for protection from the unknown and the unseen. Then, as they continued to gaze upward, a pile of hay whistled down through the hole and fell right on top of them. Linda screamed. Crawling out from under the hay, Carol and Ruby quickly tried to remove the hay from off Linda. Then, as if from nowhere, dad appeared and grabbed Linda. He lifted her out of the manger and held her close.

"It's okay. It's okay," he assured her, but what on earth are you guys doing in here anyway?" Gently he set Linda down and helped Carol and Ruby out. "Come on. I'll take you to the house."

To be escorted to the house by dad was indeed a rare privilege. Their faces showed the solemnity of the occasion. Mom noted this as well as their disheveled appearances when they entered the house.

"What happened to them?" she demanded. "Where did you find them?"

"I guess they were playing in the manger," replied Emil, "I didn't know they were there and I dumped a load of hay on top of them."

"In the manger?" repeated Erna, "In the barn?" She looked at them, suspiciously. There was guilt written all over their faces.

"Yep. Why?" Emil now also began to be a little suspicious as he looked at the three girls staring at the floor.

"They were supposed to be practicing music," said Erna. "I've been calling and looking all over for them. In fact, I was by the barn calling."

Dad saw through them. "Well Well Well!" was all he said.

"Since it's now near supper time and you girls haven't got your practicing done, you will have to practice after supper instead of going with dad for that load of hay," said Erna with finality.

All three appealed to Emil, but it was no use.

"You heard your mother."

That evening the girls practiced long and hard, and they never sang so well. Erna listened with shining eyes and a pleased expression on her face.

One day, Emil came rushing home from town carrying a special package.

"Erna, come look at this. It's from your brother."

"What?" Erna came running.

"I think it's from your brother, Emil!" He handed her the package.

Erna stared at the large envelope with unbelieving eyes. Sure enough, there was a return address on it with her brother's name. It was postmarked Argentina. With trembling hands she opened the ragged envelope. Inside she found a manuscript, a wedding picture of her brother and his wife, and a letter.

Emil helped Erna to a chair. "You'd better sit down. You're turning pale."

Erna looked at the picture for a long time. She couldn't put it down. It was Emil, her brother! He was out of the Russian prison camp. Oh how wonderful!

"Well, how about reading the letter?" said Emil.

Erna jumped at Emil's voice. She had forgotten that he was standing there. "Oh yes, the letter." Her mind had been tracing precious events in her childhood such as Emil teaching her to sing up in his loft at their farm. Her hands continued to shake as she opened the letter. It was written in German — in Emil's beautiful hand.

She smiled. Slowly she read as tears began to trickle down her face. Emil could contain himself no longer.

"What does he say?"

Erna handed him the letter and stared into space.

The letter told of his escape from prison and how he had ended up in Finland. From there he went to Argentina. While in Finland, he had gotten married. But the communists were on his trail. They tracked him down and he was forced to go into hiding, fearing for his life. His wife immediately abandoned him, probably in fear for her own life. He was now living in Argentina and hoped he would be safe there. At the end of the letter he requested money to get a new start. The enclosed manuscript contained a story he had written about what he had experienced in Russian prisons. He hoped she would publish it to tell the world what was happening to innocent people.

Erna and Emil had no money to send him. They were barely scraping by themselves. Erna explained this in a letter to him, but she never received a reply and her brother Emil was never heard from again. Perhaps the communists finally caught up to him as they did with Trotsky in Mexico.

Filled with anxiety for her brother, she made no attempt to publish his story. She herself couldn't read it because it was dictated to someone else, who wrote in a dialect unfamiliar to Erna. For years she kept the manuscript hidden. Only now, at the urging of her daughters, has she agreed to have it translated. Perhaps, as Emil had years ago requested, it will be published.

Erna belonged to an organization called the Women's' Institute as did nearly every woman in the community. The members took turns hosting the meetings in their homes. Erna's turn always brought a flurry of excitement to her household. Everyone in the family was expected to help with the preparations, while Erna bustled around issuing orders.

"Hurry girls, we have to get the center of this room cleared. Chairs all around the edge of the room. We're working on a quilt today. It will take the whole room to set up the frame."

In the middle of the room sat a huge table that had to be moved into another room. The girls grunted and struggled but only managed to get it wedged tightly in the doorway.

"Mom!" they yelled in unison.

"Oh, for goodness sakes. What next!" Erna grabbed an end of the table and heaved. It didn't budge. "Turn it a little more and then push. Ruby, you pull."

The table suddenly became unwedged and flew through the door landing on top of Ruby who screamed and then started bawling.

"Are you hurt?" asked Erna.

"No." answered Ruby.

"Then what are you bawling for?" said Erna in exasperation.

"Because the table is on top of me," complained Erna.

"Well get out from underneath it. I can't reach you."

Slowly Ruby crawled out through the table legs and out the door of the bedroom. Erna gave her a comforting hug.

Excitement filled the house as the ladies began to arrive. The quilting frame was set up and deft hands went to work. The quilt would be raffled off and the money used for those in need. The girls served the refreshments that included fancy sandwiches and treats that Erna had prepared. Erna served the coffee herself.

One of the women had a daughter that would be getting married soon. She asked Erna if she would make the cake.

Erna had become well-known throughout the community for her fabulous cakes. They were not only delicious, but they were decorated beautifully. She could design them as requested. Sometimes the requests could be pretty bazaar.

Fruit cake was her specialty and the kind most requested, but the ingredients were expensive. Erna only charged the cost of the cake, nothing for her time. Sometimes she didn't even recover her costs. Yet, she never complained.

She designed her cakes according to the colours that would be used at the reception.

As the years passed Erna began to have a lot of health problems. She suffered through many operations, the most serious of which was the insertion of a steel pin in her hip. Then there were a couple of back operations. In April, 1969 she had a disk removed from her back, scraped, and spliced back in place. She returned home from Edmonton so weak that Emil had to admit her in the Hospital at Consort.

During her stays in the hospital, her nephew, Ewald, would frequently stay at the farm to help. Emil's sister, Ella also would come to help. When they weren't available, help had to be hired. Many problems seemed to arise when Erna wasn't there, mostly with the inexperienced hired help. On one occasion a hired woman asked the girls what she should serve for meat that evening.

Ruby said, "Mom just goes out and butchers a chicken." There was lots of canned meat in the root cellar under the house and plenty of fresh meat in the storage shed but none of the girls thought of that.

"Would you girls please butcher a chicken for me then?" asked the lady.

The girls stared at each other in horror. Butcher a chicken? They had never done that before!

"We don't know how," said Ruby. "Besides the ax is too heavy for us. Can't you do it?"

"Well, I don't know how either, and what do you need an ax for?" It became very clear that she knew no more about butchering a chicken than the girls.

"To chop its head off," said Ruby.

"What?" She seemed stunned.

"They are alive you know," said Carol.

"Then I guess you'll have to get your dad to do it," said the lady with resolve.

"But he's way out in the field," said Ruby.

"So? I'm sure your legs will carry you."

"But — but —."

"Scoot, now!"

It was obvious that she didn't realize how far away Emil was, and she wasn't interested in listening to the girls.

"Don't forget to take the ax." The words echoed behind them.

Since the chickens were running freely about the yard, it took them over a half hour to catch one. Now an ax is a very heavy weapon, especially for three small girls. Being the oldest, Ruby carried the ax and Carol the struggling chicken while Linda tried to calm the doomed creature by petting it. In this manner, they started out. The girls walked and walked. The ax got heavier and heavier, the chicken never stopped trying to escape. By the time they had walked for about an hour, they were all blubbering with tears streaming down their faces.

Then they saw dad coming across the field with the tractor, the dust flying. He saw them coming and raced to meet them. Coming to a halt, he jumped off the tractor, eyeing the ax, the chicken, and of course, tear streaked faces.

"What's going on here?" he asked.

Their tears burst forth in rivers, as they all started explaining at once.

"Okay, okay. Up on the tractor, all of you. I'll take you home."

Somehow Ruby managed to hang on to the ax, and Carol on to the now exhausted chicken, and hang on to the back of the tractor at the same time. Once home, the chicken was set free and Emil told the girls to go play while he had a private discussion with the hired woman.

It was a happy day for the family when Erna returned from the hospital. Erna's girls were always her pride and joy, and, next to her husband, her greatest love. She wanted nothing but the best for them and stressed education and their "God given talents." They would finish school, no ifs or buts about it, and they would do their very best in every task that was given them, no matter how small or large it may be. They were carefully monitored to make sure they did. Erna firmly believed that love did not mean shirking responsibilities.

On a farm there is always lots of work to do. If the girls didn't know how to do a particular chore, they were taught. There were times when it would have been much easier for Erna to do a task herself than to teach the girls how to do it, but she didn't. She patiently taught them for which they would always be grateful.

Erna knew her three girls well. She knew that Ruby possessed the aptitude to be a teacher, Carol a nurse, and Linda a secretary. Farming did not figure into her plans for her girls. She did not want them to have to go through the heavy physical labor and the health problems such labor brings. All three eventually became what Erna had set her heart on their becoming.

In 1958 Ruby married George Paull. This upset Erna because she thought Ruby was too young. But, in spite of many hardships, the marriage proved a lasting one, filled with wonderful experiences.

The joy of one occasion was blunted by the tragedy of another— the untimely death of Emil's brother Oscar. His death was Probably brought about by the war that weakening his body to such a degree that cancer could take it over.

The next year, 1959, brought about two more major occurrences. Erna and Emil's first grandchild was born — a baby girl. This brought great joy to the entire family. Erna eagerly baby sat whenever the opportunity arose, and it arose often. Ruby and George would drop the baby off at Erna's and be free to go and do as they pleased. If Erna ever felt used, she never said so. She simply loved that little girl.

Then Jacob died. In spite of his domineering personality, or maybe because of it, he had held his family together and kept his farm progressing.

1960 brought the birth of another grandchild—a boy. After a series of girls, Erna and Emil were thrilled to have a boy who soon joined his sister in the baby sitting routine.

After twenty-three years of renting, Emil finally decided to buy the farm. Erna could hardly believe it really would be theirs. The transaction was made quietly, and without much ado. After all, everyone considered it their farm anyway. Erna and Emil quietly celebrated the event.

Then came the third grandchild—another girl. This one, too, was welcomed with open arms by Erna and Emil. These three grandchildren were to bring them lots of troubles and trials, but lots of love too.

Not being raised on a farm, the three grandchildren were not 'farm conscious.' They didn't know what could be dangerous, what they could safely play with, or what should not be touched. Erna had to cram years of training into a short time, which brought some interesting results.

The grandchildren loved the farm. There was so much freedom, so much to see and do, so much space in which to run. It was nothing like the town in which they lived.

One day they approached Grandma and asked if they could explore among the huge rocks in the big pasture.

"Not by yourselves." said Erna. "There's cattle in that pasture."

"That's okay. We promise not to bother them," said one.

"Yeah, but that doesn't say that they promise not to bother you."

"We won't go near them Grandma, honest," they all insisted.

"Not now," said Erna. "It's nearly lunch time." Then suddenly she had an idea. "I tell you what. I'll make us a picnic lunch and we'll all go down to the rocks and have lunch there."

The children thought that a great idea. Quickly a lunch was put together and away they went full speed.

"Don't go so fast! Grandma can't keep up," shouted Erna.

"But you said you could run real fast grandma," teased Cynthia

"Well—so I did, but I don't see any sense in getting tired before we even get there."

"We won't get tired grandma."

"No I'm sure you won't," thought Erna. Huffing and puffing, they arrived at the huge rock pile. Gleefully the children began to climb the rocks. Breathing a sigh of relief, Erna eased down on what looked like a nice smooth rock. To her utter amazement the rock split in half and she found herself lying on the ground staring at the sky. A little screech followed the fall.

The kids turned to stare. "Grandma fell!"

"No! Look! The rock broke."

"Boy, she must be heavy!" Quickly they scrambled down to help her up. By the time they got to her, she had indignantly jumped to her feet. How embarrassing, and in front of the children too! She bent over to examine the weird rock. She looked in disbelief. It wasn't a rock at all, it was a huge mushroom!

Together they inspected this extraordinary phenomenon. Erna could see that the mushroom was good to eat. Solemnly she explained to three sets of wondering eyes that some mushrooms were poisonous and could not be eaten, while others were good to eat. Carefully she tried to make them understand the difference telling them that, if you were not sure, then you didn't eat it.

Triumphantly, and with great eagerness, each child carried home a huge piece of the mushroom. They had never eaten mushrooms and were eager to try it. Over the next few days they were to eat fried mushroom, roasted mushroom, mushroom soup, mushrooms prepared in every way possible. To this day, when they see mushrooms, they remember that one and only farm mushroom!

To Erna and Emil the grandchildren always provided them with a source of deep pleasure. But they were also the cause of some very tense moments. Such occurred when Erna suddenly became aware that a strange quietness descended upon the farm. With her grandchildren around, silence was not the natural order of things.

"Emil," Erna inquired with a troubled expression, "have you seen the kids?"

"No, why?"

"Well its been awfully quiet too long for my liking."

Emil laughed. "I'll go see what they're up to." He put on his hat and went out the door. A half hour later he returned, but his usual light-heartedness did not return with him.

"I can't find them any place," he said, his voice verging on panic.

"What! You mean you haven't found them yet?"

"No! I've looked everywhere."

They both hurried out the door and began frantically shouting the children's names.

After, what seemed an eternity, they heard one little voice, "here we are," as the three prodigals emerged from behind a combine parked near the house and came running toward their very worried grandparents.

"Where have you been?" demanded Erna, "Why didn't you answer us?"

"We did, but you didn't hear us," said Cynthia.

"We were in there." said the smallest one, Crystal, who was grinning from ear to ear, despite shakes of warning from her older sister.

"You were in where?" asked Emil.

"In there." She pointed to the combine.

"Inside the machine!" Exclaimed Erna. She and Emil stared at each other in horror.

Then Erna exploded. "How could you do such a thing? Suppose someone started the machine, you'd be ground to bits."

"But we knew no one was going to start the machine." Innocent little faces simply couldn't understand such great concern.

"I don't understand how you could crawl through there anyway, with all the spikes and teeth. It's a wonder you didn't get stuck in there."

"We just about did," admitted George Jr. "It took us a long time to crawl through it." All three heads nodded assent.

"And we would never have known you were in there because we couldn't hear your!" exclaimed Erna in exasperation.

Over the next few hours the children received the lecture of their lives, one they would never forget.

Chapter 10

Lord I'll Be Home Soon

As they reached the age of sixty-three, Erna and Emil found that the farm had become a great burden. It was just too much work—too many hours of physical toil and mental strain. Since they were close to retirement age, they decided to sell the farm and buy a retirement home. It was 1971. The notice for sale of their farm, and an auction sale sent a stir of excitement and sorrow throughout the community. They would be sadly missed.

It took nearly a year to sell the farm. Erna and Emil shared many anxious moments concerning what should be done and what shouldn't. In the end a neighbour and friend bought the farm. One small piece of land was bought by another neighbour. The auction followed. Friends, relatives, and above all, the women from the W.I., group to which Erna belonged, came to help with the auction. Possessions they accumulated over a lifetime sold well and brought a good price.

It was a beautiful day with a slight nip in the air. Erna and Emil were up at dawn. Two auctioneers would conduct the sale. The younger one arrived first and began helping to set up. Friends also arrived to help. Then the phone rang.

"Yes, Erna here."

"Erna, Billy's house is on fire northwest of you. Help is desperately needed." The voice was pleading.

Instantly Erna was on red-hot alert. "Help will be on the way immediately." She slammed down the receiver and ran to find Emil.

"Emil, hurry. Billy's house is on fire."

Emil never paused, he just changed the direction he was going. "We're on our way." So saying, every man there piled into several vehicles. Erna tossed buckets, containers and heavy rags at them as they climbed aboard. In little more than an instant all the men, including the auctioneer, were gone. At a time when they so badly needed help themselves, they didn't hesitate to run to another's call for help. In spite of all efforts, the house burned to the ground anyway, but the volunteers kept the fire from spreading to the other farm buildings.

When they returned, there was already a great crowd of people at the sale and the second auctioneer was ready to start. The auction proved a great success and Erna and Emil received more than they expected. They bought a retirement home in Lacombe, Alberta near their good friends.

Before moving to their new home, the community, in which they lived most of their lives, threw a going away supper for them in the community hall to wish them farewell. A short program followed. For once Erna was not expected to make the cake. A beautiful one was made and decorated for her and Emil. At the conclusion of the event, tears flowed freely as friends said good-bye to their good neighbor.

On moving day the family was up bright and early. The weather had become colder and snow was falling. As they were downing a quick breakfast, a neighbour came to pick up the load of wheat he bought from Emil. As he drove into the yard, one of his tires went flat.

"Oh, for goodness sakes," Erna thought, "Why did he have to come today? Quickly she pushed the rude thought out of her mind. It wasn't his fault if he got a flat tire.

Then other neighbours began to arrive to help Erna and Emil move. It was the kind of thing country people just did naturally.

Lacombe proved to be a friendly town in which to live. A few days after their arrival, they were made welcome by the "Lacombe Welcome Wagon". This was Erna's first introduction to the people of Lacombe. Soon she got to know just about everyone in town. She joined the Lacombe W.I. (Women's Institute) organization and became known as, 'The Social Worker,' because she was always ready and eager to help others.

Emil did not fit in as well. He was very shy and the farm had been his whole life. Here he didn't know what to do with all his time. He went from being an over active person to an under active one. In the last few years of his life he became diabetic. Because of inactivity, the disease worsened. After having eye surgery for cataracts in 1976, he was forced to go on insulin. Erna accepted the responsibility of giving him his shots because he couldn't get around the idea of sticking the needle in himself. But try as she might, Erna could not properly regulate his insulin, because Emil couldn't seem to stick to the strict diet he required. He could not make any sense out of having to measure, weigh, and keep track of what he ate.

In keeping with his inability to monitor his diet, Erna noticed one day that his tests showed a high sugar content.

"What did you eat, Emil?" demanded Erna.

"A bit of fruit."

"That's all? You must have had something else."

"Well — I was uptown for coffee. Met some guys today." He tried to distract her from the topic. But Erna was not easily thrown off subject.

"So what did you eat with the coffee?"

He pretended he didn't hear her.

"What did you eat?" she pursued, standing directly in front of him. He couldn't ignore the question.

"I was hungry. I had a piece of pie."

"Oh Emil, you know that's loaded with sugar."

"What am I supposed to do, starve?" He became angry.

"Your going to kill yourself!" exclaimed Erna as tears welled in her eyes. The situation was really starting to look hopeless. Slowly and sadly she went to get the syringe to give him more insulin to balance the sugar he had eaten.

In January 1974 Carol married. The union was eventually blessed with two boys, both of whom thrilled Erna and Emil beyond words. But much to their regret, these grandchildren would live in the United States. Erna and Emil would not have the pleasure of seeing them often or to baby sit as they had done for Ruby's children.

In 1979, Emil began having trouble with his legs. Walking became painful. He didn't like going to doctors, so he avoided them. It wasn't until one leg turned black that he condescended to see a doctor. He was told that his blood vessels were plugging off. He would require immediate surgery on both legs or lose them. High blood sugar levels had caused the problem.

Emergency surgery was performed at the University of Alberta Hospital. His diabetes had gone completely out of control. Gradually, his wonderful doctors stabilized his condition. When he felt better, he insisted that Erna take him home. She had worked in a hospital. She could look after him, couldn't she?

He was released. Erna did her best to provide him with the care he needed, but one leg just wouldn't heal. Emil was admitted to the hospital in Lacombe where he was administered a different medicine than what he had been using. It made him very ill to his stomach. Every day Erna walked to the hospital to take care of him. Late every evening she walked home again, tired, tearful, dejected. Sometimes she was lucky and got a ride. She had never learned to drive, but now she wished she had.

Emil then suffered a serious heart attack. He was rushed to the University of Alberta Hospital in Edmonton. The attack severely damaged his heart which had become too weak to keep his lungs clear. They slowly filled with fluid. On top of that, he developed a severe rash. Not wanting to upset the family, Erna did not tell them about the heart attack or how serious Emil's condition had become. Instead she bore the burden herself. In between tears she pleaded with God not take her husband from her yet.

Her prayers were answered. Against all odds Emil began to improve. He was sent by ambulance back to the Lacombe Hospital. Soon he became well enough to return home. With family encouragement, Erna and Emil agreed to sell their Lacombe house and buy one in Sherwood Park, Alberta. There they would be close to two of their daughters and the University Hospital.

Occasionally Erna would feel a little under the weather. During those times Emil would panic and plead with her, "Don't go before me Erna. Promise you won't leave me. Promise me that."

Erna would hold him close. "I promise you Emil. I'll always be here for you."

Two years after Emil's first leg surgery he again experienced trouble with his legs. It was 1981. Two of the oldest grandchildren were engaged. They would both get married within a couple of months of each other. Emil was able to attend the first wedding, but not the second. He was back in the hospital, scheduled for a leg amputation. Several days after the wedding the operation took place. His left leg was amputated just below the knee.

The surgery was unsuccessful. They had not taken enough. Emil returned for a second operation. His heart had become weaker, but the operation seemed to be successful. He was later fitted with an artificial leg and he began therapy. Soon the doctor released him from hospital and Erna took over caring for him. It wasn't easy. He suffered constant pain which wrenched Erna's heart as she struggled through each day with him.

Then came their first great grandchild—a boy. Tears rolled down Emil's cheeks as he gently cradled the infant in his arms. Lifting it to his face, he smiled. The baby had been born nine days after his seventy-third birthday.

On July 14, Emil, having trouble breathing, was rushed, by ambulance, to the University Hospital. Five days later at six a.m., Erna got a call from the hospital asking her to come immediately. Emil was pretty bad off and calling for her. Her granddaughter Cynthia drove her there as fast as possible, but they were too late. Emil had died. Erna cried bitterly because she had not been with him during his last moments. She thought of her promise and felt like she hadn't kept it. But, her family assured her that God knows what's best for us, and this was best for her. One can only do so much.

At the funeral Erna touched her cheek to Emil's forehead in a goodbye gesture to her greatest love. "I'm coming soon, honey. I'm coming soon," was all she could whisper.

But this was not to be. God knew that she was still needed here, for her family and for others.

Erna couldn't bear staying in the depressingly empty house she had so happily shared with Emil, so she sold it to her daughter Linda and moved into a senior citizen's complex within walking distance. Being so near, she could visit Linda whenever she liked.

It didn't take Erna long to get acquainted with everyone in the complex. This greatly helped her in her loneliness. She began to frequently receive visitors.

She always left her door unlocked, so whenever anyone knocked, she'd shout, "Come in, it's open."

Purina, Erna's friend, entered one day.

"Hi Erna. Say, did you know we have a choir group in the complex?"

"A choir?" repeated Erna, her attention aroused. "No, I sure didn't."

"Yes. I heard you singing in church. You sing beautifully, and I was wondering if you wanted to join our choir. We sure could use some more members, especially someone who can sing harmony like you do."

Erna's heart pounded. Oh how she would love to sing in a choir again, but she hadn't sung for so long. Could she really sing again?

"Well, I don't really know. I think I'm kind of old for that now."

"You're no older than the rest of us in here. Come on, we really do need you."

"I suppose I could give it a try."

"Excellent! See you at the next practice." Erna's visitor left.

Joyfully Erna hopped around her small apartment. She was going to sing again! It was the first real taste of happiness she had felt in a long time.

She joined the choir and was delighted to learn that it sang at senior citizen residences throughout the area at various functions that encouraged elderly people to get out and participate in group activities. This led to many opportunities for Erna to help others. She began to fill up her hours, to diminish her loneliness, and get on with her life.

One day a friend barged into her apartment without bothering to knock on the door. She was very excited.

"Hey, Erna," she called after catching her breath. "Did you know they're going to record us tonight?"

"What do you mean, record us?"

"They're going to make a tape of us where we'll be singing tonight. We will be able to buy copies of it."

"That sounds great! but I don't have a tape recorder."

"Well buy one."

"No, — I never could figure those things out, but I probably will get a tape anyway as a souvenir. Maybe the kids will play it."

Erna sang with the choir for over ten years. She quit when she had to leave her little apartment and move to a senior's lodge.

Forever independent, Erna could not bear to sit around waiting for her children to take her places, so she began to explore the bus systems. This led her on many adventures. One evening Ruby phoned her and was greeted with a very down sounding hello, instead of her usual cheery voice.

"What's the matter, mom? Are you sick?"

"No, I'm not sick!"

"You sure sound sick."

"I'm just awfully tired."

"How come? What did you do now?"

"Oh, nothing."

"Yes you did, or you wouldn't be so tired. Come on, tell me."

"I just took a little bus ride."

"Good for you! Where did you go?"

"Well, I kind of got lost."

"You got lost? On the bus?"

"I thought I was getting off at this shopping center but it turned out to be the wrong place."

"So what did you do?"

"Seems I rode several wrong buses, and got quite a unique tour of Edmonton. Anyway, I finally got on the right one, but by that time I was too tried to go shopping, so I decided to come home. Only the bus I took was the wrong one, so I had to get off and wait for another. When it arrived, I discovered I'd left my purse on the one I had just got off of. To make a long story short, I have my purse back and I'm safely home."

"Oh, for goodness sakes mom!"

"But I do know which buses to take now."

"You mean your going to go again?"

"Well of course! What do you think!"

And so Erna became an expert on public transportation. She was always gone exploring here or there. A lot of time was spent visiting various hospitals. If there was someone there she knew, she would be sure to visit them to try to help them, or cheer them up. Many would be the elderly from her apartment complex.

Her ability to use bus transportation helped cast her in another roll—that as guide. It all started when one of the residents asked Erna if she would be taking the bus to the hospital one day.

"Sure am. Why?"

"Can I go with you? I never could figure those buses out. You seem like you know all about them."

Erna laughed. "Well, I can't say I know all about them, but I have had my experiences with them. Sure, I'd love to have you come with me. I'm leaving in about an hour."

From then on Erna helped others use public transportation.

Whenever she came upon a task that needed done, she assumed the responsibility of doing it without being asked or expecting anything in return.

Noticing the vast number of plants throughout the complex that seemed neglected, Erna began watering them on a regular basis.

When news got around that she was looking after the plants, many of the tenants put their plants in her care and were grateful for the way in which the plants thrived and provided an atmosphere of health and beauty.

Some of the residents would try to tell Erna how to look after certain plants. She would listen with great interest and then continue to do as she pleased. The plants never looked so good. This was to be Erna's job for many years until poor health prevented her from doing it any longer.

Erna, like her older sisters, was an accomplished seamstress. She had made most of her girls' clothes when they were little. She continued to sew, do embroidery work, and other needle craft in her new apartment. She was now, however, much slower at it, due to severe eye problems, but the beautiful, neatly done stitches were still the same. She donated many items of sewing and baking to their senior's craft and bake sales. The money was used for things needed in and around the complex, or for those in need.

One night from a sound sleep, Erna sat bolt upright. "What was that horrible sound?" she thought. Quickly she put on her hearing aid and heard what seemed to be a whistle. She turned the hearing aid up a bit. No, it was the fire alarm! Heading for the door, she grabbed her housecoat and wrapped it tightly around her. In the hall a lady in a wheel chair waited for the elevator. Erna knew this was wrong. Under no circumstances do you enter an elevator during a fire.

"Wait, you can't go down on that," said Erna.

The woman turned a deathly white face to her. With pleading eyes she said, "I have no other way of getting down. I can't walk."

"Come on, I'll help you."

"I'm too heavy for you. You can't help me."

Erna realized the woman was right.

"I'll get you some help."

By now they had been passed by several other residents, heading for the stairs.

Quickly Erna pushed the wheel chair toward the stairs and grabbed the arm of a man in the hallway.

"Please, this lady needs help. She can't walk."

The man paused, looked at the two women, and then jerked his arm free. He hurried away without a word. Erna then stopped two people, a man and the strongest looking woman she could see.

"Please, we need help. This lady can't walk."

The pair hesitated only briefly. Then the three of them carried the lady in the wheelchair down the stairs to the lobby where other residents were milling about in confusion. Tears streaming down her face, the woman in the wheelchair gave Erna a big hug of gratitude.

The building manager appeared and called for their attention.

"Ladies and gentlemen, your attention please. Please don't go outside in the cold unless we give you notice. We don't believe we have a fire, but the fire truck will be arriving soon to investigate. Move to the sides and allow room for the firemen to get through."

As the fire truck screamed to a halt, a path was made for the firemen. After what seemed a long two hours, the residents were allowed to return to their apartments. Erna seen to it that management helped the lady in the wheel chair back to her apartment. It was later learned that a small fire set off the alarm. What caused the fire was never revealed to the residents. For a long time after, Erna slept with her hearing aids on.

Erna's activities were somewhat curtailed with the development of severe osteoporosis. This debilitating disease caused her to suffer a collapsed vertebrae and fractures on her spine, resulting in her experiencing acute pain. Her doctors could do nothing but prescribe pain killers while the fractures healed.

In 1995 she suffered another fracture so serious that she had to be hospitalized. Even in her pain she tried to keep up her sense of humour.

One day, a nurse tending Erna, in an attempt to make small talk said, "Erna, you sure don't look eighty-six years old."

"Well, you can't tell how far a frog can jump by his looks, and I sure can't jump very far."

The nurse laughed. "We are going to get you back jumping again. You just wait and see."

"I doubt it. Think my jumping days are over."

"You never know. We're pretty good in here."

"You probably are, but no matter how good you are you have to have reasonable material to work with."

"You look like pretty good material to me."

"As I said, you can't —."

"I know, tell how far a frog can jump by his looks," the nurse finished her sentence. Then she laid a pair of leg braces on the bed. "Now Erna, the first step toward jumping again is to learn how to use these braces. When you have accomplished that, you will be scheduled for therapy. It will be tough, but I'm sure you will do just fine."

Erna looked dubiously at the ominous silver supports on her bed. She wasn't even sure that she had the energy or the will to get moving again. How could these nurses, how could anyone, know the pain she suffered? Even the pain killers didn't seem to work. She felt like giving up. Why couldn't she give up? Why did she have to endure this? Why? Unnoticed, tears slipped down her cheeks as she quietly whispered, "Dear Lord, please take me home."

Soon the therapy began. It was to prove very frustrating. Erna couldn't do what she wanted to do and the pain was excruciating. She cried bitter tears of hopelessness and disappointment.

One day Ruby and her husband dropped in for a visit. Erna's first words were, I've got to get out of here. They tell you that you can do it, then they think just because they told you so, you can. They make me so tired. It's so painful."

Ruby put our arms around her mother's shaking, shoulders and tried to calm her.

"You will, you will come home, mom," Ruby assured her, just as soon as you are a little more mobile. Then you can come home with us."

"I don't know that I want to go home with you guys."

"Why not?"

"I'll just be a trouble to you. Linda said I could come home with her too. I told her no too."

"But you can't go back to that apartment by yourself, mom. You have to come with us. You won't be any more trouble than we have been to you in the past."

Always a jokester Ruby's husband George tried to change her mood. "Guess you'll just have to get up and do the two-step around this bed with me."

"I don't think I can even do the one-step, let alone the two-step." But she did smile.

And she did get back on her feet, using a four wheeled cart to help her walk. She began to travel up and down the hospital corridors.

Nurses looked at each other and smiled.

"Hey Erna, are you a good driver?"

"You bet I am! See I even have a license." She pointed to her name tag on her cart.

"Just be careful you don't get any speeding tickets."

"You sure don't have to worry about that." Erna laughed. It was good to here her laugh again.

After being released from the hospital, Erna went to live with Ruby and her family. An ambulance brought her to the door. Ruby had prepared a spare bedroom for her and brought some of Erna's furniture and other belongings from her apartment to make her feel more at home.

Then began a conflict of wills. Erna's medication, a sizable amount, had to be dispensed according to the doctor's instructions. Erna was used to taking her own medicine, when and if she felt like it, and in doses she deemed necessary. It is not easy to take 'bossing' as Erna called it, from anyone, let alone your own daughter, especially for someone who had always been as independent as Erna. Her doctor (Dr. Cahill) was called in to run interference. This wonderful man would come to see Erna where ever she was.

Erna's strength and vitality gradually returned. Even though she wanted to go back to her apartment, in her heart she knew it was not possible. Yet she desperately wanted her independence. To that extent a room was found for her in a Senior's Lodge. This meant that she had to get rid of most of her possessions. She worried about who would want her 'old junk,' as she called it. She then discovered her children, grandchildren, and great-grandchildren did indeed want her things. She had a wonderful time deciding who would get what, and then giving it to them.

Adjusting to the Lodge was hard. She could no longer do her own cooking. She had to eat with everyone else. Yet even here she was on the alert for ways to help others. The dining room was composed of many tables, each seating six people. A conflict arose at one of the tables because one woman coughed so much, the others no longer wanted her at their table.

Erna was appalled.

"She can sit at out table," insisted Erna, "I cough a lot too."

"Thanks Erna, but I'm afraid she can't," said Maureen, one of the attendants.

"Why can't she?" demanded Erna, "We still have room."

"Because we have a new couple coming in a few days and I've already designated your table for them." The staff lady walked away before Erna could put up any objections. The Lodge had to be run by stiff rules in order to take proper care of its occupants.

It is a lovely place run by very caring people. The Canadian Government subsidizes its expenses. Nursing help is readily available for those needing it. A variety of activities are made available to any interested residents. Performing groups frequently come to entertain. Regular church services are held on Sundays. Erna found a marvelous, loving evangelical pastor leading one of these services. His concern for the elderly extended far beyond what was expected. He is always available to help any that want his help.

Erna is content, as she waits for the day she will see her Lord and Emil again. She has never failed to put flowers on his grave for father's day and his birthday. She hasn't forgotten him and keeps track of each wedding anniversary.

Erna continues to zoom down the Lodge corridors with her little cart. One can even imagine puffs of smoke coming out from under her feet and the cart wheels as she goes. She will not slow down. Others get out of her way and let her pass. Even her constant pain doesn't stop her.

All of her children and grandchildren are grateful for all the lessons Erna taught them. They are grateful for her faith, love, strength, endurance, and devotion to her family.

Epilogue

At 89, Erna resides in a nursing care home in Sherwood Park. Her mind is still keen, but her back confines her to a wheel chair. Still undaunted, she zooms down the corridors. Dr. Cahill tells us that she barrels down the hallway like a bullet. “Maybe you should talk to her.”